A TASTE OF COWBOY

A TASTE OF
COWBOY

RANCH RECIPES AND TALES FROM THE TRAIL

KENT ROLLINS

WITH SHANNON KELLER ROLLINS

PHOTOGRAPHS BY SHANNON KELLER ROLLINS

A RUX MARTIN BOOK
HOUGHTON MIFFLIN HARCOURT
BOSTON   NEW YORK   2015

Copyright © 2015 by Kent Rollins and Shannon Keller Rollins
Photographs copyright © 2015 by Shannon Keller Rollins
Photograph on page 185 © Greg Payne

For information about permission to reproduce selections from this book, write to
Permissions, Houghton Mifflin Harcourt Publishing Company, 215 Park Avenue South,
New York, New York 10003.

www.hmhco.com

Library of Congress Cataloging-in-Publication Data
Rollins, Kent.
   A taste of cowboy : ranch recipes and tales from the trail / Kent Rollins with Shannon
Rollins ; photographs by Shannon Keller Rollins.
   pages   cm
"A Rux Martin book."
ISBN 978-0-544-27500-3 (hardback) — ISBN 978-0-544-27318-4 (ebook)
   1. Cooking, American—Western style. 2. Ranch life—West (U.S.) 3. Cowboys—West (U.S.)—
Social life and customs. I. Rollins, Shannon. II. Title.
TX715.2.W47R686 2015
641.5978—dc23   2014036936

Book design by Endpaper Studio
Typeset in Bodoni Six

Printed in the United States of America
DOW 10 9 8 7 6 5 4 3 2 1

DEDICATION

---◆·◆·◆---

THIS BOOK IS DEDICATED TO THE TWO MOST IMPORTANT women I've ever known and loved, women who believed in me and told me to always believe in myself and never give up on my dreams.

My mother, God rest her soul, was a saint and taught me to love, to care, and that it's okay to be a soft man. She taught me to trust my instincts, and to never forget my upbringing, my faith, and, most of all, my goals. She fed us when times were lean and the groceries were leaner; but no matter what, both our stomachs and our hearts were full. Thanks, Mama, for your love, for your dedication, and for teaching me that it's not only important to have good food at the table, but also family.

To my sweet wife, Shannon. My gosh, I love you. Your dedication and inspiration are priceless. You made me believe in myself again. It's your love that keeps me going day after day. You have been beside me in conditions that would make most people run off and hide: heat, smoke, wind, and hours of work. Your beauty is not only on the outside, but also on the inside. For someone who told me early on "I don't cook," you have come a long way. Thanks for your vision, your writing, your editing, and your cooking. I know I'm lucky to have you, and a better partner I could never find, both in life and in business. There are a lot of important things in life, but in mine you're at the top. I've always said, "A man is only as strong as the woman who holds him, and I'm the strongest man in the world."

ACKNOWLEDGMENTS

———◆·◆·◆———

THERE AREN'T ENOUGH PAGES IN THIS BOOK TO THANK all the folks who have made this journey possible. Like a good steady horse, they helped get me to this destination.

My mother and dad, Wash and Joy Rollins, who have both passed on. They taught me more than just cooking. They taught me life.

All the cowboys whom I've fed through the years. They were the best food critics I've ever had. They ate my food for weeks at a time and were always hungry and appreciative.

The chuck wagon cooks who did this for a living when living was harder to do. They braved the hours, the elements, and the smoke with blood and sweat. Thank you for paving the way.

Janis Donnaud, our publishing agent. Some folks you meet once and know they are good people. She believed in me and guided us through this whole process. None of this would have been possible without her.

Rux Martin, Laney Everson, and the rest of the crew at Houghton Mifflin Harcourt Publishing. Thanks for giving this cowboy the opportunity to share my lifestyle with the world.

Lisa Diercks and George Restrepo of Endpaper Studio, for re-creating our world in the book's design.

Donnette Engebrecht, also known as the "Comma Queen." Thanks, Honey, for the hours of proofreading and, most importantly, for your friendship and love.

Beth Schiff, for introducing me to Skype and always believing in me.

Charissa Melnik, for never asking me to be something I'm not.

All the old-timers I was raised around. Men who stood as tall as giants and were the best role models ever, and all the women I grew up around and who shared the smells and tastes from their kitchens. Your inspiration is priceless.

Hollis, Oklahoma, the rural community I was raised in, which always made me mindful to cherish the little things in life.

CONTENTS

INTRODUCTION

HOWDY, AND IF I COULD FOLLOW that with a handshake, I would. I like a good handshake and looking someone in the eyes; in my circle those two mean a lot. I'm a cowboy, a cook, a writer, a dishwasher, and a purveyor of words that sometimes rhyme. I've cooked for legends and those that were just legends in their own minds. I've got more friends than I will ever have money, and I know which to value the most. I've been in places you can't see from the road or even find on a map. I've even cooked food I can't spell.

My kitchen isn't typical. It has no thermostat and there are no knobs on anything that might be considered an appliance. I've cooked in every condition known to mankind, except an earthquake. I've had so much exposure at times it hurts, but it ain't the kind of exposure you might be thinking of. I've been exposed to sunburn, windburn, and frostbite. I'm a chuck wagon cook.

Now you may be asking, "What is a chuck wagon cook?" Well, it sure isn't glamorous by any stretch of the imagination. There have been times it's been 117 degrees outside before I even built a fire, and times it's been cold enough that you could hang meat. I remember when Bobby Flay came to challenge me to a throwdown of chicken-fried steak. It was a mild 97 degrees with a roaring fire. As sweat was dripping off his face he asked me, "Why would anyone do this?!" I told him it was for the job security, because no one else was crazy enough to do it.

Even though the modern age has crept up on us, the chuck wagon is still used today on some ranches to feed cowboys. From eating a lot of bad food off wagons and having taught myself how to cook in Dutch ovens while helping my uncle guide hunters in the Gila Wilderness of New Mexico, I knew I could do better. So in 1993 I bought an 1876 Studebaker chuck wagon and slowly started my business, catering for friends and family and then for local ranchers when they worked their cattle. Soon word got out about the great food and business was booming. Today my wife, Shannon, and I travel all across the country feeding hungry folks for everything from birthday parties to bar mitzvahs. I've also made television appearances on the Food Network's *Throwdown! with Bobby Flay, Chopped: Grill Masters,* and *Chopped Redemption* and on NBC's *Food Fighters.* More importantly, I maintain the tradition of cooking from the chuck wagon for cowboys on true working ranches during the spring and fall.

One of the talents of the wagon cook, in addition to creative cooking, is the ability to move. Now, I wish I were talking about moving like James Brown, but I'm talking the U-Haul kind. Depending on the ranch, we may set up camp made of teepees and the wagon for a few days, and then pack up and move to another pasture to work more cattle. I've moved camp to a different spot as often as once a day. This can be tricky when you not only have to worry about packing, but feeding a hungry crew too. I've stayed

Cowboy cooking is made from ingredients you'll already have on hand such as potatoes, cheese, canned beans, and onions.

anywhere from one day to five-and-a-half weeks out on a ranch and seen all seasons pass through in one day.

But I'm truly a lucky man, because I get to feed cowboys. Every time I step out of my teepee to go fix breakfast for a crew, I'm carrying on a tradition and reliving history. The view out my office window doesn't look onto skyscrapers, and you can't catch a cab where I work, but you can catch dinner as it comes slithering through camp. I've cooked up some rattlesnake hors d'oeuvres good enough for any city slicker's palate. Food doesn't get any fresher than that!

What I cook and the way I cook are real, simple, and authentic. Those are the three things that have always meant the most to me. A meal can be as simple as drinking a good cup of boiled coffee from the wagon with good friends. My mother taught me to

put love into my cooking and prepare dishes that make you feel good when you cook them and better when you serve them. A smile and full stomach have always gone a long way for me. I think the world today needs a good recipe for values, sprinkled with a little common sense, along with good eats. I had those recipes growing up. They were dished out in generous helpings from folks who knew nothing but hard work and helping others.

I remember when I was on *Chopped,* folks asked me which chefs inspired me the most to cook. Well, I certainly wasn't influenced by any "celebrity" chef. The chefs I look up to don't have fancy titles—they are known as Mama, Aunt, Neighbor, and Friend.

Cowboy cooking is made from ingredients you'll already have on hand such as potatoes, cheese, canned beans, and onions. You won't need to saddle up and ride to the store to pick out some foreign food you can't pronounce that they had to fly in from a far-off country—like California. We cowboys have evolved a little from the beans and jerky that those fellers had to exist on long ago, but the simplicity is pretty much the same.

Many of my recipes involve canned ingredients. When I'm out on the wagon for five weeks, or if the ranch headquarters is seventy miles from the nearest town, fresh fruit and veggies aren't abundant. A common misunderstanding is that canned can't

be good. When Chef Aarón Sánchez ate my food on *Chopped*, he said, "Kent made refried beans with chipotle that had tons of smokiness and heat. He transformed them and made me forget they were canned."

I've cooked for and cowboyed on different ranches across New Mexico, Kansas, Texas, and Oklahoma. And with that comes a lot of tales of where I've been and what I've seen. I've had to chop ice to make coffee water, been in dirt storms so bad that I had to light a lantern in the middle of the day, and been in rain so heavy I had to cook below the undercarriage of the wagon. The stories I share in this book are important because they represent the authentic cowboy way of life and describe characters whose personalities and adventures color the West. They're rooted in morals that both a cowboy and a CEO can relate to and learn from—they're honest and straight shooting. Everyone I've met has shared some wisdom, and I'll share it with y'all too.

If the food or stories don't transport you to my camp, then surely the pictures will. Take a tour of the wagon and see the art of Dutch oven cooking, meet fellers like Brother Daniel and his dogs, smell the coffee ole Bertha is brewing up, and hear those cows bellering. I hope *A Taste of Cowboy* will be a journey for you into the pastures I've been to, so you can see the faces I've seen and the fires I've built.

So, let's saddle up and ride out—we're burning daylight!

> NOTE: You can do like I do and use Red River Ranch Seasoning in place of salt and pepper in many recipes in this book. Order Red River Ranch Original Seasoning and Red River Ranch Mesquite Seasoning from www.kentrollins.com.

THE CHUCK WAGON:
THE FIRST MEALS ON WHEELS

THE INVENTION OF THE CHUCK wagon is credited to Charles Goodnight around 1866. Goodnight needed a way to feed cowboys who were moving contrary Longhorn cattle up a trail. One of the most famous of those trails was the Chisholm Trail, which ran from near San Antonio, Texas, to Abilene, Kansas. According to history, Goodnight converted an old Studebaker army freight wagon into the first chuck wagon, so named because "chuck" was slang for food.

By removing the grain boards from the back of the wagon and replacing them with a box, Goodnight created a portable kitchen. Like all kitchens, chuck boxes vary, but they are typically composed of shelves and drawers for holding necessities. It was usually stocked with flour, a little sugar, beans, a few spices, coffee, and maybe a little jerky. The compartment under the chuck box, called the "boot," held pans, Dutch ovens, and skillets.

The chuck wagon had to be strong and tough enough to cross thick country and rivers; many had to forge their own trails. It hooked up to a team of mules or draft horses and was driven by the cook. It generally rode ahead of the cattle herd for two main

reasons: so the cook could get far enough ahead to be able to fix a meal before the cowboys got there and to keep from getting caked with dust. (You can imagine how much dirt two thousand Longhorns can kick up.)

Days were long and nights were short. Cowboys were usually fed two meals a day, consisting of coffee, beans, and biscuits. Not unless a steer died were they fortunate enough to eat much meat, other than a little salt pork. Their job was to *move* the cattle, and the boss man sure wouldn't be happy to know the cowboys were eating his profits.

When it came time and there was a town close by the route, the cook would restock the wagon and gather any other supplies he might need. In the mid to late 1800s, after all, Walmart wasn't just around the corner. The cook had to know how to plan a menu and what supplies he would need for the long journey.

The cook was usually a grumpy feller and often just as stubborn as the team of mules he was driving. But you can imagine, with the harsh conditions and limited supplies, he might be a little ill-tempered. I once heard an old-timer say, "That old cook looks mean and nasty but don't judge him at first glance 'cause he might be cooking your next meal." No one ever questioned the cook because he was second in command behind the owner or manager, and he was the boss at the wagon. On top of being a cook, he was the doctor, dentist, counselor, and mechanic.

He mended broken limbs, stitched up wounds, and pulled teeth when the occa-

The cook was usually a grumpy feller and often just as stubborn as the team of mules he was driving.

sion arose. His coffee was always hot, and he never ate until the last man was fed. There were a set of rules that applied to a cow camp: You don't eat till the cook calls "Chuck." Don't ride into camp, or you'll kick up dust around the cook and his surroundings. Don't spit under the wagon tarp or smoke there unless you've been given permission. The spot between the fire and the chuck box is sacred ground, and no one passes through it except the cook.

Just like old Cookie, I too have worked in some of the harshest conditions. From hailstorms to heat waves, dust storms to blizzards—you have to keep the wood dry and the coffee hot . . . no matter what.

I still have the same rules, and most of the time the hands abide by them. I have stitched up a feller or two, not with horsehair like old Cookie might have used, but with dental floss soaked in alcohol. The groceries are a lot better now, but the conditions and the transportation are still the same. Some of the ranches my wife, Shannon, and I cook on even use the same camps they used 150 years ago. It goes to show that no matter how far we've come, we can still follow the tracks of our ancestors.

Like I tell folks, we are the luckiest people in the world. We get to do what we love every day and feed real cowboys. So hop on the wagon and let's go, 'cause those fellers are expecting supper.

COWBOY LINGO

Buckaroo, vaquero, cowpoke, cowpuncher: A cowboy. "Buckaroo" refers to cowboys in the Great Basin region and parts of California. *Vaquero*, Spanish for "herder of cattle," originated in Mexico and then moved north to California. "Cowpoke" and "cowpuncher" are generic terms loosely used across the country.

Buffalo chips: When wood was scarce along the trail, the cook would pick up buffalo or cow patties and burn them. They put out an intense heat but burnt out quickly.

Bull calf: A male calf that hasn't yet been castrated.

Calf: A young bovine prior to weaning.

Cavvy, remuda: A band, or group, of

horses brought along on a *works*. These are working horses that are used to gather, rope, drive, and sort cattle. Typically, a cowboy will use three to five horses, depending on the length of time of the works. "Cavvy" is the term typically used by *buckaroos* in the Great Basin region.

Chapping (pronounced "shapping")*:* When a group of cowboys takes a pair of *leggings* and whips them over the backside of another cowboy while he is held down. This is usually done in good fun when a cowboy's birthday is revealed, but it can also be used as a harsh tactic when a cowboy is out of line and needs an attitude adjustment.

Chaps (pronounced "shaps"), **leggings, chinks, woolies:** The leather worn by cowboys to protect their legs in rough and/or brushy country. "Chinks" are shorter, usually knee length. "Woolies," typically made of goat or sheep wool, are worn in extremely cold climates for the warmth.

Cookie, Cusinero, Coosie, Hash Slinger: Names for a chuck wagon cook.

Cow: A female that has borne a calf and is used for reproduction.

Cowboy hat crease: The shape of a cowboy's hat, which can be a representation of geographical location and also personal style. Numerous styles exist, including the "flat brim" worn by *buckaroos* in the Great Basin region or the "taco crease" often seen in, but not limited to, Central Texas.

Cow camp: The location where the wagon and teepees are set up during a *works*.

Dogie/doggie (pronounced "*dough-ghi*")*:* A motherless calf.

Dude: An inexperienced or wannabe cowboy, typically with little or no ranching experience.

Heifer: A young female that has not borne a calf.

Jingling: When a bell is placed around a horse's neck so the cowboys can hear where the herd is during the dark early-morning hours.

Kack, **wood:** A saddle.

Opossum belly: A piece of cowhide secured to the underside of the wagon, used for hauling wood and cow or *buffalo chips*.

Pulling out the wagon: A time, typically in the spring and/or fall, when the wagon is moved to feed cowboys while they are working cattle at different locations on a ranch.

Punchy: A cowboy way of doing things.

Slick: A yearling calf that has not been worked (branded, vaccinated) because it was missed on a drive when cowboys were gathering cattle.

Slicker: A plastic or canvas long coat worn in wet weather.

Steer: A male that has been castrated.

Tapaderos or taps: Leather or rawhide cover on the stirrups to protect the boot from thorns and cold weather.

Teepee, range teepee: Typically secured with two poles hinged at the top. Many are rubber floored with a zippered door. These are a different style than Indian-made teepees.

War bag, riggin' bag: A canvas or leather bag packed with the essentials a cowboy will need during a *works*.

Works, gather: The time, typically in the spring and/or fall, when cowboys are working cattle. Spring duties include vaccinating, branding, castrating, and ear-tagging. Fall duties include weaning, vaccinating, and catching any missed calves from the spring.

IN KENT'S KITCHEN

Bertha: She's been with me a long time. I've loved her, kicked her, cussed her, and even threatened to throw her off into the Mississippi River. But just like that old chuck wagon of mine, she's never let me down. She's my camp stove and an all-purpose kitchen unit. I had a feller make her for me in 1993 'cause I got tired of digging a hole and having dirt blow in the gravy. She weighs 385 pounds and can reach temperatures unknown to NASA. She doesn't have many friends in July but when it cools off, she's a pretty popular ole gal.

Biscuit cutter: I don't have anything fancy in my kitchen, but I'm sure even Martha Stewart would be proud of this particular item. I have discovered the best biscuit cutter is a green chile can with the top and bottom cut out.

Chuck box: Located at the back of the wagon, this is the cook's kitchen. It is usually built with drawers and shelves and carries all the essentials any kitchen may have. A lid pulls down and serves as the counter.

Cream cans: Two large galvanized cans that formerly were used to carry milk from the barn to the house. I now put flour and sugar in them, and they're secure enough that a mouse can't get in.

Fly, wagon sheet: The canvas tarp that covers the area behind and over the wagon for protection and shade.

> No one should come into the cook's kitchen unless they are invited—especially if it is early in the morning.

Gourd dipper: A hollowed-out gourd used for dipping water from the barrel.

Hash knife: Talk about your all-in-one, multipurpose kitchen tool. I'm not talking about a fancy food processor. This knife is a slicer, a dicer, a chopper, and a scraper. I've even used it to get the ice off the windshield. Traditionally, the hash knife was used to cut up meat and vegetables to make a stew or hash.

Medicine box: Every kitchen has that one miscellaneous or junk drawer. Mine has medicine and a first-aid kit in it. I always keep a little dental floss there because I once had to stitch up a cowboy with the floss soaked in alcohol after he got into a battle with a mesquite tree.

Shovel with holes: I took a flat shovel and drilled holes through it, which allows the ash to sift through. Ash insulates and doesn't cook so it's important to have plenty of coals when baking in Dutch ovens.

Trivets: Although most Dutch ovens are made with legs, they don't really offer much of a heat buffer when the oven is placed on the coals. Trivets help raise the oven off the ground and farther from the coals to help regulate the heat. I have short and tall ones depending on what I'm cooking and how hard the wind is blowing.

Water barrel: A thirty-five gallon-wooden barrel made of oak and secured with leather to the side of my wagon.

Wreck pan: Usually a galvanized tub that is used for washing dishes. I have two that sit under the water barrel; one for washing with soap and one for rinsing.

CAST IRON CARE

CAST IRON HAS BEEN AROUND FOR a long time and, if it's taken care of and treated with respect, it will outlive us all. Nearly all of my cookware is made out of cast iron, from Dutch ovens to skillets. If it was good enough for all those old cooks going down the trail, then it's good enough for me.

Cast iron has many benefits. It emits no toxic fumes while cooking, it is oven safe, it helps to flavor food, it is sturdy, and it can actually help boost iron intake. I would much rather absorb iron than Teflon, wouldn't you?

Seasoning is extremely important and will make all the difference.

Seasoning New Cast Iron

First of all, if you are in the market for buying new cast iron, buy American made. There are a lot of bad cast iron pieces made overseas out of a lot of trash materials, which can cause cookware to warp and cook unevenly.

Most new pieces of cast iron bought today are preseasoned. Since I don't know how they seasoned it, I always use my own method for new pieces or older pieces that have been restored.

Rinse out the cast piece with warm water. Use the soft side of a sponge to wipe out any residue. Place the piece on a burner over medium heat. (Warming the piece opens the pores in the cast and allows it to accept the seasoning.) Wipe out any excess moisture with a clean rag and let the heat evaporate any remaining moisture. Remove from the heat. Place a dab of olive oil on the inside of the piece. You don't want an oil slick because this will create a buildup. I prefer to use olive oil when seasoning because vegetable oils can become rancid over time. As the old-timers used to say, "It will help your cast to taste sweet." Rub the olive oil around with a clean, lint-free rag. Never use paper towels on cast iron because they will leave lint, which will eventually build up.

Place the piece on a cookie sheet and rub the outside with any cheap oil, since it won't affect the taste of your food. The cookie sheet will prevent oil dripping off the piece and onto your oven, causing it to smoke. Place the cookie sheet in an oven heated to 200°F. Leave in the oven for 30 minutes, then turn off the oven and let cool. Repeat this step two or three times. Remember, you only need to do this method on *new* cast iron.

The best things to cook in newly seasoned cast iron are potatoes and bacon. These will help create flavorful seasoning on your cast iron.

Cleaning and Preseasoning Cast Iron

Never use soap on cast. Simply rinse the piece out with warm water and scrape any residue out with a wooden spoon or a sponge. Once your piece is clean, be sure to reseason after every use. Place the piece over medium heat until the moisture disappears. Place a dab of olive oil on the inside and wipe with a clean cloth. Depending on use, I typically season it two times a year

with cheap oil (vegetable or canola), but I season Dutch ovens more often since they get outdoor use.

For particularly sticky situations, fill with warm water and let soak. A cobbler that has burned in a Dutch oven can create a sticky mess. Often, I put the Dutch oven or skillet in an open fire and let it sit just long enough to release the stuck food. You can also do this in the house by turning your oven to "self-clean" and leaving the Dutch oven in there until the burned portions begin to release. The cast piece will then need to be reseasoned on a burner over medium heat (see page 15).

Rust Care

The best cast iron ever made was Griswold. You can still find some pieces at antique shops and estate sales. If they are rusty, or if you have any rusty pieces of your own, don't give up on them. If you have true, well-made cast iron, it can be brought back to life. The best things for cast iron are heat and oil; anything else can be potentially harsh.

I place a rusty piece of cast in an open fire and allow it to thoroughly heat up, about 15 minutes. Then I remove the piece and scrub it with a wire brush. I repeat this method several times, adding a little oil after the first few times to see how the rust is coming out. Sometimes, rust lives deep down in the pores and this can be a long process,

The only time you should fear cast iron is if your wife is fixin' to hit you with it.

but you have to remember, it didn't get like that overnight.

You can also try this method in your oven by setting it on the self-cleaning setting. If you have extremely old pieces or pieces that are very thin from use, this may be a better method than the fire.

If the heat and oil process doesn't work, you can also warm the cast over a fire or a burner at medium/high heat, add coarse salt, and, with a piece of leather or glove, buff out the rusty spots. The salt will help remove the rust. Be sure the cast is warm while doing this.

My last resort is vinegar. You can use the salt with vinegar and even a little baking soda to make a paste and rub the cast with it. I've even soaked pieces directly in the vinegar. This is a quicker method but can be caustic to the cast.

After you remove the rust, follow the procedure for seasoning new cast iron to restore it.

Storage

Be sure to store cast iron in a dry place. When storing Dutch ovens, place a paper towel between the lid and the oven. This will act as a wick and allow air to circulate and prevent the oven from souring. If you live in a humid climate, you can also sprinkle a little Minute Rice in the bottom to absorb the moisture.

Threats to Cast Iron

EXTREME TEMPERATURE CHANGES: Heat and cold will not hurt cast iron unless it is exposed quickly to extreme temperatures. Especially if you're cooking outdoors, gradually warm and cool cast iron to prevent it from cracking.

ACIDIC FOODS: Foods containing acid and sugars, such as barbeque sauces and cobblers, can be particularly hard on cast. That's why it is important to properly clean and season after every use.

BOILING WATER: I never boil water in my seasoned cast iron. Boiling water will cause the seasoning to release and turn the water, or whatever you're cooking in it, black. If I cook beans, I make them in a polished cast pot that I only use for boiling beans. Some folks boil water to clean their cast. Don't do this: Boiling removes some of the much-needed seasoning.

SOAP: My mother put her Griswold cast iron skillet into the dishwasher every night after supper. I told her that the soap would eat the seasoning and cause food to taste bad. But you sure aren't going to tell an eighty-year-old woman what to do, so I got used to the taste of Cascade. Water is all you need to clean cast iron.

THE STUDEBAKER—
MY PORTABLE COWBOY CARETAKER

LONG BEFORE THEY MADE AUTO-mobiles, Studebaker built wagons. From buggies to freight wagons, the company played an important role in molding our history.

The Studebaker brothers built their first wagon in 1852, and by the late 1880s, they had grown into the largest horse-drawn vehicle builder in the world. Their success was largely due to the military contracts they received during the Civil and Spanish-American wars. During the latter, the company was contracted to deliver five hundred wagons within thirty-six hours, which they accomplished.

Horsepower takes on true meaning in a Studebaker. The teams I have driven have pulled the wagon over some rough country: uphill, downhill, across rivers, and down dirt roads that haven't seen a wagon wheel in a hundred years. If we have to move camp more than once or twice, a team of horses or mules takes the wagon around the ranch. Otherwise, we haul the wagon in on a trailer and set up camp.

We pull the wagon up to a designated spot, unhitch the team, and set up camp.

We try to carry enough groceries in to last about a week at a time. There's no Frigidaire, so we pack in a lot of canned goods and nonperishables. A good ice chest is our refrigerator, and someone makes the trip from the ranch headquarters to camp to replenish the meat and ice every few days. Each camp has a woodpile for cooking. On the larger ranches, one cowboy is in charge of a particular camp and is responsible for stocking the wood in that area. I've burned everything from a cedar post to a cow chip—anything to get the food hot and the cowboys fed.

The farthest I've driven the wagon with a team in one day is seventeen miles. This may not seem like much, but in a wagon going about three to five miles an hour, it is a long haul. Wagons are stout, but they sure weren't made with shock absorbers or fancy upholstered seats. I feel every hump and holler in the road. But for me, this is still the best means of transportation. There's nothing more relaxing than driving a wagon with a good team pulling it. A slower pace of life is often the fastest way to cure your problems.

JINGLING THE HORSES
(BREAKFAST)

IT'S THE START OF A NEW DAY, AND I HOPE, FOR YOUR SAKE AND SANITY, that yours doesn't begin as early as mine does when I'm cooking on a ranch. Most of the time, in the spring and fall, Shannon and I wake up around 3 or 4 A.M. You heard me right: It ain't brunch, and it's way before the rooster crows.

I always set an alarm, but I don't think it's ever actually woken me up. That old clock in my head goes off automatically. After I climb out of my bedroll and stumble to the kitchen, the first thing to do is stoke my stove, Bertha, and she gets that life's blood to boiling: Coffee has always been the first thing on and the last thing off in Cookie's kitchen.

Chris Morton will usually be the first one from the crew to come over to the wagon, a man as tough as boot leather with a heart of gold. We discuss the day, as well as solve the problems of the world. As time inches closer to breakfast, more cowboys trickle in from the comforts of their teepees. I can always count on fellers to be early at the beginning of spring or fall works, but as the weeks go by, the weary cowboys can barely get there in time to eat.

Before breakfast, it's tradition that two of the hands will round up the remuda, the band of horses, to then rope out the day's mounts. Each cowboy typically brings two to four horses depending on the length of the works. Some are better for long rides, and some are better for sorting cattle. And just like a spare tire, there is a replacement in case of an injury.

The night before, the cowboys tie a jingle bell to one or two horses and then the whole remuda is turned out into a pasture or trap for the night. The next morning, when it is usually still dark, the boys listen for the jingling and know where the horses are grazing. They then gather them up and place them in a set of pens. Each cowboy chooses a particular horse he will use that day and ropes it out.

Many outfits still use the traditional jingle bell, especially operations with a lot of land. However, some ranches today gather the horses in the late afternoon or early evening to sort out the next day's mounts. The mounts are then placed in a pen so they don't have to be sorted in the morning. While some operations don't use the jingle bell anymore, the term "jingling" is still used to describe the gathering process.

When the fellers take off in the morning to jingle the horses, I finish preparing breakfast for all the crew. When they make it back to camp, we have a prayer and then breakfast. Then it's back to the pens for those boys to saddle up and get ready for their commute to work. All I know is, their bellies are full, and they're fit to do battle with land and cattle.

THE RECIPES

BLUEBERRY LEMON MORNING CAKE

PREP TIME: 15 MINUTES
TOTAL TIME: 1 HOUR AND
15 MINUTES
MAKES 1 BUNDT CAKE
(12 TO 16 SERVINGS)

---

2 cups blueberries, fresh or frozen

3 cups all-purpose flour, plus ½ cup if using frozen berries

1 teaspoon baking powder

1 teaspoon salt

2 sticks butter, softened

2 cups sugar

3 large eggs

1 cup lemon yogurt

1 teaspoon vanilla extract

Zest of 1 lemon

Powdered sugar for sprinkling

Blueberries are one of my favorites in the morning, and this is a tasty way to use them in a breakfast or brunch treat. But we never did have "brunch" where I came from—that's just something sleepy folks call breakfast. This is a moist cake with a citrus twist and jam-packed with blueberries.

1. Preheat the oven to 350°F with a rack in the middle. Butter and flour a Bundt pan.

2. If using frozen blueberries, toss them in a small bowl with ½ cup of the flour and set aside. If the blueberries are fresh, skip this step.

3. In a medium bowl, combine the 3 cups flour, the baking powder, and salt. Set aside.

4. In a large bowl, cream the butter and sugar together for about 1 minute, or until fluffy.

5. Beat in the eggs, one at a time. Mix in the yogurt, extract, and lemon zest.

6. Slowly mix the flour mixture into the wet mixture until combined. If using frozen berries, sift the flour out. Fold the sifted frozen berries or the fresh berries into the batter. Scrape the batter into the Bundt pan.

7. Bake for about 1 hour, or until a toothpick inserted into the cake comes out clean.

8. Remove from the oven and let cool. Run a knife around the edges of the cake to loosen. Place a plate on the bottom and flip the cake over onto the plate to remove. Sprinkle with powdered sugar and serve at room temperature.

COWBOY BREW CAKE WITH CREAM CHEESE ICING

PREP TIME: 10 MINUTES
TOTAL TIME: 35 MINUTES
MAKES ONE 9-X-13-INCH CAKE
(ABOUT 15 SERVINGS)

2½ cups all-purpose flour

I teaspoon baking powder

½ teaspoon salt

I stick butter, softened

1½ cups sugar

½ cup light brown sugar

I large egg

2 tablespoons sour cream

½ teaspoon cinnamon

I cup strong coffee, cooled

2 tablespoons used coffee grounds

I tablespoon maple syrup

Cream Cheese Icing
(recipe follows)

Coffee is the life's blood of cowboys. It's the first thing on and the last thing off the stove in my camp. We also drink quite a bit from that ole Mr. Coffee at home, but there's usually a little left over in the pot. Shannon and I got to thinking what we could do with the remaining coffee, and before our brainstorming was plumb over, we even had a purpose for the used coffee grounds. Stir it all in to make a sweet cake that turns out incredibly moist with a hint of coffee. Top with an easy icing that has the subtle hint of coffee to enhance the morning flavors.

1. Preheat the oven to 350°F with a rack in the middle. Butter a 9-x-13-inch cake pan.

2. In a large bowl, combine the flour, baking powder, and salt. Set aside.

3. In a medium bowl, beat together the butter, sugar, and brown sugar.

4. Slowly beat in the egg, sour cream, cinnamon, coffee, coffee grounds, and syrup until well combined.

5. Slowly beat the wet mixture into the dry mixture for about 1 minute, or until combined.

6. Pour the batter into the cake pan. Bake for about 25 minutes, or until a toothpick inserted into the center comes out clean.

7. Let the cake cool slightly before cutting. Spread the icing over the top and serve warm or at room temperature.

CREAM CHEESE ICING

PREP TIME: 5 MINUTES
TOTAL TIME: 5 MINUTES
MAKES ABOUT 1 CUP

1 (8-ounce) package cream cheese, softened

¾ cup powdered sugar

¼ cup strong coffee, cooled

1 teaspoon honey

½ teaspoon vanilla extract

1. In a medium bowl, beat the cream cheese until smooth.

2. Beat in the remaining ingredients until well combined.

BROTHER AND HIS COFFEE

◆ ◆ ◆ ◆

ABOUT SIX YEARS AGO I WAS IN THE Palo Duro Canyon in Texas. Every year, at the 5R Ranch, we would set up camp the Sunday after Thanksgiving and stay three weeks, give or take a couple of days. It would always be cold, and a calm day would have twenty-five-mile-per-hour winds. This particular gathering brought a new character into camp by the name of Brother Daniel, a cowboy by trade and by birth. He was a simple feller who didn't speak too many words, except to his dogs and horses.

Brother would set his teepee up pretty close to the wagon and me. He said it was so he could hear the coffee pot in the morning. Brother did like his coffee. He would go to bed around 7 P.M. and be waiting for me to build a fire the next morning at about 3 A.M. Now according to camp etiquette and the cowboy code, no one should come into the cook's kitchen unless they are invited—especially if it is early in the morning. But for Brother that was two hours too late!

At about 2 A.M., I would hear Brother a fussin' and cussin' at Jo Jo and Pete, his two dogs who were his roommates, telling them to quit growling and not to crowd him so bad. As soon as I would get a lantern light burning, I could hear his teepee unzip and those spurs jingling. Now I like to have a little quiet time in the morning, and the first time I heard Brother heading my way, I turned the lantern out. Brother would nearly get to the wagon, and when the light went out, he would head back toward his teepee. I would hear the zipper go up, and he'd say, "Go back to sleep, you two. It ain't ready yet."

Well, this went on for three or four more times, until I finally gave in and turned the lantern up bright. When Brother came in, he said, "You need to work on that lantern, Cookie, I can maybe fix it so it will stay on if you'll let me." I just chuckled to myself and told him, "I think I got it going."

Brother and I shared many a cup of coffee warmed by Bertha and many a story over those long, cold three weeks. He told me about the ranches he'd been on in Montana and Nevada and all the different country he'd seen up north. He described the horse wrecks he'd been in and when he broke his ankle bad enough that the bone was sticking plumb through the skin. We never talked much about women, because the biggest loves in Brother's life were his dogs and cats. A simple feller he was and that's why he touched my heart the way he did. Brother had all he needed: a teepee, a warm bedroll, two sleeping roommates, and a lantern.

I sometimes forget, on occasion, the

simple things in life. To me the things folks take for granted mean the most. When you don't have modern conveniences like electricity and running water, you get by, and sometimes, you get by even better. The world we live in today is sure enough in a hurry, and you can get run over every day if you're not careful.

So take some advice from Brother and me: Slow down when you can, appreciate what you have, and savor the moment just like a good cup of coffee.

ANGEL FLAKE BISCUITS WITH CHOCOLATE SYRUP

PREP TIME: 15 MINUTES

TOTAL TIME: 1 HOUR AND 15 MINUTES

MAKES 18 TO 22 BISCUITS

2½ cups buttermilk

1 (¼-ounce) package rapid-rise yeast

3 tablespoons warm water

¼ cup sugar

1 tablespoon baking powder

1 teaspoon baking soda

1 teaspoon salt

⅓ cup vegetable oil

4½ to 5 cups all-purpose flour

½ to 1 stick butter, melted

Chocolate Syrup
(recipe follows; optional)

We always had these biscuits with chocolate syrup on Christmas morning. We knew they were special, and they were nearly better than getting presents. It's probably my favorite biscuit, because of its rich butter flavor. When Mama made these, I would ask her why they were called Angel Flake, and she told me, "Because when you drench them in heavenly butter and then fold them back over, it's like an angel folding her wings to rest. The wings form a bond of love, and there's a lot of love in these biscuits." By love, I think she meant butter. Just make sure to use plenty of both when making these.

1. Lightly butter a 9-x-13-inch baking pan or a 12-inch cast iron skillet.

2. Pour the buttermilk into a large bowl.

3. In a small bowl or measuring cup, dissolve the yeast in the warm water. Mix the yeast mixture into the buttermilk. Whisk in the sugar and let sit for 1 minute.

4. Whisk in the baking powder, baking soda, salt, and oil. Slowly stir in enough flour to form a soft dough that is no longer sticky.

5. Turn the dough out onto a floured surface and roll out to ¼ to ½ inch thick. Cut out using a biscuit cutter. (You should get 18 to 22 biscuits.) Gather up the scraps, roll out again, and cut.

6. Pour the melted butter into the baking pan or skillet. Dip both sides of one dough round in the butter and fold in half, like a taco. Place the biscuits in the baking pan or skillet close together and repeat with the remaining rounds.

I've never had to decorate a plate to get someone to eat it. If your food is good enough, they will eat it off a shingle.

7. Place a piece of buttered wax paper over the biscuits and let rise in a warm place for about 40 minutes, or until nearly doubled in size.

8. About 20 minutes before baking, preheat the oven to 350°F with a rack in the middle.

9. Uncover the biscuits and bake for about 20 minutes, or until golden brown.

10. Serve warm, drizzled with the chocolate syrup if using, or with your favorite biscuit fixin's.

CHOCOLATE SYRUP

PREP TIME: 15 MINUTES
TOTAL TIME: 15 MINUTES
MAKES ABOUT 2 CUPS

1 cup sugar

2 ½ tablespoons unsweetened cocoa

¾ cup water

1 stick butter, cut into chunks

1 teaspoon vanilla extract

TIP: You can make the syrup ahead of time; just be sure to warm before using.

This syrup is a rich blend of cocoa and sugar. Add a slab of butter and watch the two blend in melted happiness.

1. In a medium saucepan, whisk together the sugar, cocoa, and water. Cook over medium-high heat until the sauce comes to a boil, whisking constantly.

2. Add the butter to the cocoa mixture. Whisk in the vanilla.

3. Allow the mixture to come back to a rolling boil. Boil for 3 to 5 minutes, whisking constantly, until the mixture thickens just slightly.

A lady told me, "I guess the cowboy is a dying breed." I told her, "No, Ma'am, you just can't see him from the road."

SOURDOUGH BISCUITS

PREP TIME: 15 MINUTES
TOTAL TIME: 1 HOUR AND
40 MINUTES
MAKES ABOUT 16 BISCUITS

1 (¼-ounce) package rapid-rise yeast

3 cups Sourdough Starter (*page 34*)

4 to 5 tablespoons sugar

⅓ cup vegetable oil

2½ tablespoons baking powder

2 teaspoons salt

2½ to 3 cups all-purpose flour

2 tablespoons butter, melted

Sourdough was a staple in old cow camps because milk and buttermilk were hard to come by on the trail. Along with beans and coffee, biscuits were about all a cowboy was going to get. This started out as Grandma's recipe that I tweaked so they turn out light and fluffy. The biscuits have a sweeter and softer sourdough flavor than traditional San Francisco sourdough. Be sure not to overwork the dough. Like I always say, the only time I "knead" biscuit dough is when I'm broke!

1. Preheat the oven to 350°F with a rack in the middle. Butter a 9-x-13-inch baking pan or 12-inch cast iron skillet.

2. In a large bowl, dissolve the yeast in the starter. Whisk in 4 tablespoons of the sugar and let sit for 1 minute.

3. Whisk in the oil, baking powder, and salt. At this point, taste the starter. If it is too tart, add a little more sugar, to taste. Remember, the first time you use the starter, it will be the sourest.

4. Slowly begin stirring in the flour until it makes a soft dough and is no longer sticky. Turn the dough out onto a floured surface and roll out to about ½ inch thick.

5. Cut out about 16 rounds with a biscuit cutter and place on the baking pan or skillet close together.

6. Cover the biscuits with a buttered piece of wax paper and let rise in a warm place for 40 minutes to 1 hour, or until nearly doubled in size.

7. Uncover the biscuits and bake for 20 to 25 minutes, or until golden brown. Brush with melted butter and serve warm.

SOURDOUGH STARTER

PREP TIME: 5 MINUTES
TOTAL TIME: 12 HOURS AND 5 MINUTES
MAKES 8 CUPS

---

4 cups warm water

1 (¼-ounce) package rapid-rise yeast

5 tablespoons sugar

4 cups all-purpose flour

1 russet potato, peeled and quartered

Sourdough is like my old hat; it has many uses and fits in a lot of different situations, from biscuits to pie-crusts to battering meat. You can even substitute it in any recipe that calls for milk or buttermilk. This sourdough is a tad sweeter and a whole lot easier to keep than most. Traditional sourdoughs are like needy horses. You have to feed them, read them a bedtime story every night, and feed them again. But you won't have to feed this one constantly, and it's ready to go in twelve hours. It was a staple for old Cookie on the trail, and it's still used on my wagon today.

1. Add the warm water to a crock jar that holds at least 1½ gallons. This will prevent the starter from frothing over while it's setting up.

2. Whisk in the yeast and sugar and let sit for 1 minute.

3. Slowly whisk in the flour. Drop the potato pieces into the bottom of the crock jar. Cover with a tea towel and let sit on the counter for at least 12 hours, stirring halfway through. You can let the starter sit longer for a more sour flavor.

4. Before using the starter in a recipe, whisk it briskly until smooth.

TIP: The starter will be sourest with its first use, so you may want to add a little more sugar to the first recipe you use it in.

I typically keep this starter for a week at a time, stirring at least once a day. However, you can keep it as long as the potato stays intact. I prefer to use a russet potato because it holds up the best, but you can use any potato you have on hand. Always cover the starter with a towel and never refrigerate it.

RECHARGING THE STARTER

1½ cups warm water

1½ cups all-purpose flour

1½ tablespoons sugar

When you have used 3 cups of the starter, whisk all the ingredients into the jar. The starter is ready to use again, or you can let it sit for 6 to 12 hours to create a more tart taste.

Back in the wagon trail days, the cook would sleep with his crock of sourdough starter to keep it active. I never did like my starter that much.

ALL-NIGHT SOURDOUGH PANCAKES

PREP TIME: 10 MINUTES
TOTAL TIME: 20 MINUTES
MAKES ABOUT 10 (4-INCH) PANCAKES

2 cups Sourdough Starter (page 34), briefly whisked before measuring

1 large egg

2 tablespoons vegetable oil

2 tablespoons sugar

2 teaspoons baking soda

1 teaspoon salt

1 teaspoon vanilla extract

½ to ¾ cup all-purpose flour

Butter and maple syrup for serving

Get yourself a strong cup of coffee, 'cause you'll be up all night making these. Well, that's not true, but you could tell folks that if you want them to think you slaved over their breakfast. Usually all-nighters make your head hurt, but this recipe does all the hard work for you. Make your sourdough starter the night before, and while you're sleeping, it will be making your breakfast. These are a nice change from your regular ole buttermilk pancakes. You'll get a tangy sourdough flavor with a little sweet too. By the time you cover them with a slab of butter and syrup, your tongue will slap your teeth wanting more.

1. In a large bowl, whisk together the starter, egg, oil, sugar, baking soda, and salt. Let sit for 1 minute.

2. Whisk in the vanilla. Slowly begin stirring in the flour until it reaches a pancake-batter consistency.

3. Heat a large skillet over medium heat. When the skillet is warm, coat it with butter or cooking spray.

4. Pour the batter onto the skillet in batches, making about 4-inch pancakes, or use a ¼-cup dry measuring cup. Cook until bubbles begin to form and the undersides are golden brown. Flip and cook the opposite sides to golden brown. Serve warm with butter and syrup.

Usually all-nighters make your head hurt, but this recipe does all the hard work for you.

SOURDOUGH CINNAMON ROLLS

PREP TIME: 15 MINUTES
TOTAL TIME: 1 HOUR AND
20 MINUTES
MAKES 8 TO 10 ROLLS

3 cups Sourdough Starter
(page 34)

1 (¼-ounce) package rapid-rise
yeast

½ cup plus about ⅓ cup sugar

1 teaspoon salt

⅓ cup vegetable oil

3½ to 4 cups all-purpose flour

½ to 1 stick butter, melted

2 tablespoons cinnamon, or
to taste

Brown Sugar Icing
(recipe follows)

Cinnamon rolls are always a favorite, and now you can add a twist to them with that sourdough starter you've got sitting on the counter. It makes a light dough that fluffs up even more while baking.

1. Preheat the oven to 350°F with a rack in the middle. Grease a 12-inch cast iron skillet.

2. In a large bowl, whisk together the starter, yeast, ½ cup of the sugar, the salt, and vegetable oil. Let the mixture sit for 1 minute.

3. Slowly stir in enough flour to form a soft dough that is no longer sticky. Turn the dough out onto a floured surface and roll into about a 12-x-18-inch rectangle (¼-inch thick).

4. Evenly pour or brush the melted butter onto the dough. Sprinkle the cinnamon and about ⅓ cup of the sugar over the buttered dough and lightly rub around the top of the dough. Use your judgment on how much butter, cinnamon, and sugar to use.

5. Beginning at the long side of the rectangle, tightly roll up the dough. Cut the roll into eight to ten 1-inch-thick pieces.

6. Place the rolls in the pan. Cover with a buttered piece of wax paper and let rise in a warm place for 40 minutes, or until nearly doubled in size.

7. Uncover the rolls and bake for 20 to 25 minutes, or until golden brown. Drizzle with the icing and serve warm.

BROWN SUGAR ICING

PREP TIME: 5 MINUTES
TOTAL TIME: 5 MINUTES
MAKES ABOUT 1 CUP

¾ cup light brown sugar

⅓ cup heavy cream

2 tablespoons butter, melted

1 teaspoon vanilla extract

Whisk all the ingredients together in a small bowl until smooth.

Anyone can fry meat and boil coffee, but a great Dutch oven cook is one who can bake bread and desserts in all conditions.

A YEAR IN HIS BOOTS

A COWBOY DOESN'T HAVE A TIME card to punch, and he is always on call. Holidays are limited and the hours are long. It's like an old-timer once told me, "A cow don't own a calendar and don't know anything about days off!"

Our busy time of year kicks off during what's called the "spring works," which, depending on geographical location, can start as early as February or as late as June. It's a time made up of long days, short nights, and many an hour in the saddle. The purpose of spring works is to gather up the cattle that have been out grazing and brand, vaccinate, and tag them. Grazing pastures can vary greatly in size, and some of the bigger outfits have a single pasture the size of one feller's entire ranch. The smallest ranch I've ever cooked for was 20,000 acres and the largest nearly 300,000. It's safe to say you don't see much of this cowboy's work from the interstate.

The cowboy's morning starts early. He usually crawls out of his bedroll around 4 or 5 A.M. He has breakfast at the wagon, saddles up, and bounces his backside into the early morning light, helping to spread a line across the pasture to push the cattle toward a set of pens.

The calves are separated from their mamas by cowboys on the ground and on horseback and left in the pen. Then it's time to build a branding fire and get those irons hot! At least one mounted cowboy begins roping the calves and dragging them near the fire, where the ground crew vaccinates and fly-tags them to prevent disease, notches their ears, and brands them to identify which ranch they belong to. In addition, the male calves are castrated. When the calf is small there is minimal bleeding, and within a matter of minutes, it is up and back to the herd.

After the calves have been worked, all the cattle are released. The cowboys form a circle, called "holding the herd," to let cattle settle and the mamas to pair back up with their calves. This ritual takes place in each pasture throughout the ranch until the entire herd has been gathered and worked.

Summer brings a somewhat slower pace for the cowboy, but there are still fences to fix, windmills to check, dietary supplements to administer, and the occasional sick or crippled yearling to doctor.

Before you know it, the season is changing again, and it's time for fall works, which can stretch from August to December. The cowboys gather the herd in again and give fall inoculations, pull fly tags (the fly-repellant tags), and check the cows for

pregnancy. The calves are weaned from their mamas and usually trucked or pushed on horseback to another part of the ranch and turned out to graze in fall pastures. The cowboy checks this herd frequently because the stress of being weaned can cause sickness in yearlings. When this herd is ready, they are loaded up on trucks and shipped to a feed-lot or auction barn.

Winter is just around the corner, which means the cowboy or rancher begins to feed the cattle more, due to colder conditions and the lack of grass. The feeding schedule is weekly, and chopping ice off of frozen ponds or tanks so the cattle can

drink is a daily chore. There are no snow days or calling in sick.

Next comes calving time, which can begin as early as December or as late as May. First-time mothers, called "springing heifers,"

"A cow don't own a calendar and don't know anything about days off."

may have to be assisted at birthing time. Just like an on-call doctor at the hospital, the cowboy gets little sleep. By the time all the cows have calved, it's spring again and time to start the whole process over.

NEW YEAR'S POOR MAN'S SAUSAGE

PREP TIME: 10 MINUTES

TOTAL TIME: 16 MINUTES

MAKES ABOUT 6 PATTIES

⅔ cup all-purpose flour

½ teaspoon red pepper flakes

¼ teaspoon sage

¼ teaspoon celery salt

⅛ teaspoon ground cumin

1 (15.8-ounce) can black-eyed peas

2 tablespoons chopped yellow onion

1 large egg, beaten

Bacon grease or vegetable oil for frying

TIP: These are best cooked in bacon drippings for more flavor.

It is traditional in my country to eat black-eyed peas on New Year's Day for good luck in the upcoming year. Now I ain't too sure about luck, because as the old-timers said, what's going to happen will happen, and if you're in the right spot, it won't hurt. But I'm not one to stray from tradition. The origin of this type of recipe is from the Great Depression and Dust Bowl. My dad told me meat was so hard to come by then that you felt like a one-winged chicken hawk just trying to survive. There were many meat substitutes back then. I've added more seasonings like cumin and red pepper for a bolder flavor, but I'm sure I make it with the same amount of love the Greatest Generation made it with back then, just trying to get by.

1. In a medium bowl, combine the flour, red pepper, sage, celery salt, and cumin. Set aside.

2. Using a colander, drain the black-eyed peas. Scrape them into a medium bowl and mash with a spoon. Stir in the onion and egg.

3. Scrape the mixture into the flour mixture and mix well with your hands.

4. Lightly flour your hands. Spoon about a 2-tablespoon-sized dollop into your hands and pat into about a 3-inch patty. Repeat with the remaining mixture.

5. Pour enough grease or oil to cover the bottom of a large cast iron skillet and heat over medium-high heat.

6. When the grease is hot, place the patties in the skillet and cook until golden brown, 2 to 3 minutes per side, mashing slightly. Let cool slightly on a paper towel or rack. Serve warm.

CREAMY WHITE GRAVY

PREP TIME: 8 MINUTES
TOTAL TIME: 8 MINUTES
MAKES ABOUT 2 CUPS

½ cup bacon, sausage, or other meat grease

5 tablespoons all-purpose flour

1½ to 2 cups milk, warmed

Salt and black pepper

TIP: A lot of times on ranches I use canned milk, which gives a very rich flavor, but sometimes I add a little water to thin it. You can also use heavy cream for a richer taste.

I remember watching Mama and all those old women whip up batches of gravy with three simple ingredients: grease, flour, and milk. Gravy scares some folks, like my wife. Don't give up on a batch of gravy: You can always bring it back with a little more milk or flour. And be sure to give it enough salt and pepper. Whip this up for breakfast and serve with Sourdough Biscuits (page 33), or for an evening meal with mashed taters.

1. Heat the grease over medium heat in a large cast iron skillet.

2. Sift in the flour and let it come to a boil for 2 minutes, stirring and mashing down constantly with a flat spatula.

3. Slowly stir in 1½ cups of the milk and bring back to a light boil. Continue stirring until the mixture is smooth and reaches the desired consistency, about 2 minutes. You can add more milk or water to thin the gravy, if necessary.

4. Season with salt and pepper to taste. Serve hot.

I've sat a lot of mornings around the wagon and listened to the darkness – silence often speaks with great volume.

COWBOY COFFEE

PREP TIME: 15 MINUTES
TOTAL TIME: 15 MINUTES
MAKES ABOUT 10 CUPS

¾ cup coffee grounds

TIP: I use 2-gallon coffee pots, which hold about 1½ cups grounds and 1½ cups cold water. You can also use a saucepan if you don't have a graniteware coffee pot. Feel free to adjust the coffee grounds measurement and length of boiling to suit your taste.

It may be hard to believe, but my most requested recipe is for coffee. Folks can't get over how smooth it is. I've had people tell me they haven't been able to drink coffee because of their acid reflux or sensitive stomachs, but they're able to drink mine. The secret is in the boiling. Boiling takes the acid out of the bean and makes it smooth. The trick to settle the grounds is to pour a little cold water down the spout.

1. Fill a 3-quart graniteware coffee pot with water to the bottom of the spout.

2. Place the pot over high heat and allow the water to warm. When the water has warmed, pour in the coffee grounds.

3. Let the water come to a good roiling boil. Reduce the heat to medium and let boil for 2 to 3 minutes. Be careful the water doesn't boil over. Remove the pot from the heat and let sit for 1 to 2 minutes. Pour ½ to ¾ cup of cold water down the spout to settle the grounds. Serve hot.

THAT OLD BLACK MAGIC

A COWBOY WILL TELL YOU GOOD coffee is not only a necessity but a given at the wagon. It's the first thing on the fire in the morning and the last thing off every night.

There are all kinds of coffee-making gadgets nowadays. The spitting, spewing drip coffee maker often sounds as loud as our beagle snoring at night. There's the percolator, the French press, and the fancy ones that make a fast cup at a time, but try that at the wagon, and you'll get a chapping. For me it's my old reliable graniteware coffee pots: no gadgets, knobs, beeps, or spits—just good boiled coffee.

Sometimes I forget what a mysterious thing good cowboy coffee is to some folks. But I'm reminded every time Shannon and I cook for a festival or catering event. People can be a little skeptical when they come by looking at my well-worn pots, but once they try the coffee, they are hooked. They can't believe how smooth it is. I just look at them and say, "It's boiled coffee, but we can boil it another hour and call it Starbucks!"

At a festival one day, a feller got a cup of coffee, came back for a few more refills, and kept assessing the situation. I finally went over to him and asked, "Your coffee all right, sir?" He replied, "I have to tell you I'm a coffee snob. I am so particular about my coffee that I have to import beans from Venezuela to get the right kind. Yours is incredible, so I must ask, where do you import your coffee from?" I knew it was going to break the poor feller's heart when I told him Walmart, and that I always serve Folgers.

You could see the agony on his face. "I don't drink Folgers!" he exclaimed. "Well, sir, you just drank about six cups," I answered. We had a good laugh about it, but it just goes to show that you don't need gadgets, gizmos, or high-priced beans to have a good cup.

Part of the secret to a flavorful taste is also due to my well-seasoned pots. Just like my cast iron, they've never seen a drop of soap. I simply rinse them well with hot water, which helps build a good seasoned taste. So get to making yourself some of this black magic, 'cause I guarantee you there's nothing better than a good cup and a good sunrise to start the day.

LEON GOES TO CHURCH

I'VE BEEN BLESSED TO MEET A LOT of good folks from cooking on ranches and traveling the country catering. A very special person and someone I call a dear friend is a man by the name of Leon. He is a fifth-generation cowboy, and, if you look up "cowboy" in the dictionary, Leon's picture should be there.

He is one of the most devout Christians I've ever been around, but surprisingly, he's never set foot inside a church. Leon would tell me, "You know, Kent, the pew I sit on is my saddle. The pulpit I hear a sermon from is my saddle horn. That's where I feel closest to God, just sitting there on horseback."

Well, it was several years ago that Leon had to move off the family ranch, near Mountainair, New Mexico, to a smaller place in Elida due to health concerns. It was hard for him to leave the ranch that he had lived on forever. He called me up and asked if I wouldn't mind helping him and his wife, Darla, move things from his old ranch.

When I pulled up to their house in Mountainair, I noticed Leon had two black eyes. Leon is not a man to fight, so I couldn't figure out what might have happened. When I got out of the truck, I asked him, "Leon, where'd you get those black eyes?" "You ain't going to believe this, Kent. I got them in church." Well, I knew I had to hear this story.

Leon went on, "I was bringing seven yearling bulls out of that pasture on the backside of the ranch, and you know that little country church that sets just across the road? I heard the most beautiful music coming out. Well, I just decided I'd leave them bulls there and go into that church. I took off my hat and my spurs, so I wouldn't be making no racket, and found an open spot in the back. Well, as soon as I got settled, the preacher said, 'Ya'll stand and we'll sing Hymn 368.' Now, Kent, it was really hot in that church and I noticed that a tremendously large woman was standing in front of me. Due to perspiration, her dress had gathered there on her in a most unbecoming spot. I thought to myself, I'll help this poor woman out. So ever so slowly, I plucked her dress out of where it had stuck. When I did, that woman swung around and clocked me right there in the eye!"

"Well, Leon, that explains the one black eye, but what happened to the other one?"

"Kent, I just cowboyed up, 'cause she didn't want it out of there, so I just pushed it right back in!"

SKEETER'S SAUSAGE CASSEROLE

PREP TIME: 20 MINUTES

TOTAL TIME: 7 HOURS AND 50 MINUTES

MAKES 6 TO 8 SERVINGS

6 large eggs

3 cups milk

2 tablespoons mayonnaise

1 teaspoon powdered mustard

1 teaspoon salt

½ teaspoon black pepper

3½ cups seasoned croutons

2 cups shredded cheddar cheese

2 cups (about 12 ounces) chopped sausage links, cooked

1 (10.5-ounce) can cream of mushroom soup concentrate

This little dish is one of the creations of my father-in-law, Steve, also known as Skeeter. It can be made for any breakfast, but it's a special-occasion dish that we serve every Christmas morning. It's one of those head-start dishes where you do the prep work the night before and then slap it in the oven the next morning. It cooks up into a fluffy, moist casserole and includes everything a breakfast should in one dish: meat, cackle berries (the cowboy's term for eggs), and gooey cheese. Croutons, the secret ingredient, create a flavorful crust.

1. Lightly butter a 9-x-13-inch casserole dish.

2. In a large bowl, whisk together the eggs and 2½ cups of the milk. Whisk in the mayonnaise, mustard, salt, and pepper.

3. Spread the croutons on the bottom of the casserole dish. Sprinkle the cheese and sausage evenly over the croutons. Pour the egg mixture over the casserole.

4. In a small bowl, whisk together the remaining ½ cup milk and the soup concentrate. Spoon heaping teaspoonfuls of the soup mixture evenly on top of the casserole. Cover and place in the icebox for at least 6 hours or overnight.

5. Rise and shine, it's sausage time! Preheat the oven to 350°F.

6. Uncover and cook the casserole for 1½ hours, or until it is bubbling and heated through. Serve warm.

BREAKFAST EGG BOWLS WITH SMOKY CREAM SAUCE

PREP TIME: 15 MINUTES

TOTAL TIME: 40 MINUTES

MAKES 5 SERVINGS

1 (5-count) can refrigerator biscuits

5 tablespoons butter

5 large eggs

5 pieces thick-cut bacon

Smoky Cream Sauce (*recipe follows*)

This breakfast is better than one from the drive-up window because you get all the essentials in one bite. It's easy to throw together using canned biscuits. The real star—the sauce—makes it a special treat.

1. Preheat the oven to 350°F with a rack in the middle. Butter 5 cups of a muffin pan or five 7-ounce ramekins.

2. Place the biscuits on a floured surface and roll out to ⅛ to ¼ inch thick.

3. Place the biscuits in the muffin cups or ramekins, pushing the dough up the sides and slightly over the top edges.

4. Place 1 tablespoon butter in each of the cups and crack an egg into each.

5. Bake for about 25 minutes, or until the biscuits are golden brown.

6. Meanwhile, in a large skillet, cook the bacon over medium heat until crispy, about 10 minutes.

7. When the biscuits are done, remove from the pan and crumble 1 piece of bacon over each of the egg bowls.

8. Drizzle with the cream sauce and serve warm.

TIP: If using a jumbo-sized biscuit, bake in the 7-ounce ramekin or jumbo muffin pan and increase the baking time about 10 minutes.

SMOKY CREAM SAUCE

PREP TIME: 5 MINUTES
TOTAL TIME: 10 MINUTES
MAKES ABOUT 1 ³/₄ CUPS

1 ½ cups (12 ounces) cream cheese, softened

6 tablespoons milk

2 teaspoons Worcestershire sauce

1 teaspoon smoked paprika

¼ teaspoon cayenne pepper

A sauce should complement a dish, not mask it or cover up a mistake. This sauce goes with these breakfast bowls like a saddle on a horse. The smoky cream cheese with a pinch of cayenne will give a kick-start to your morning.

1. Mix all the ingredients together using a food processor or electric mixer for about 1 minute, or until thoroughly combined.

2. Pour the ingredients into a small saucepan and heat over medium-low heat, stirring constantly, until warmed through, about 5 minutes.

FIVE-LAYER FIESTA WITH GREEN SAUCE

PREP TIME: 25 MINUTES

TOTAL TIME: 25 MINUTES

MAKES 6 SERVINGS

6 to 8 tablespoons oil for frying

6 Ore-Ida frozen hash brown patties (from a 27-ounce box)

1 (16-ounce) can refried beans

6 large eggs

1½ to 2 cups crumbled queso fresco or shredded mozzarella cheese

Green Sauce (*recipe follows*)

Five layers of crispy hash browns, refried beans, cheese, fried eggs, and green sauce come together for an early morning feast. The sauce offers just enough bite to tickle the taste buds.

1. Preheat the oven to 200°F. Lightly butter a baking sheet.

2. In a large skillet, heat 3 to 4 tablespoons of the oil over medium heat. Add 3 or 4 of the hash brown patties and fry until golden brown, 7 to 8 minutes per side. Repeat with the remaining patties, adding additional oil if needed. Set on the baking sheet and put in the oven to stay warm.

3. In a medium saucepan, cook the beans over low heat, stirring occasionally, until warmed through, about 5 minutes.

4. Meanwhile, in the hash brown skillet, fry the eggs until over-easy to over-medium.

5. Spoon about 2 heaping tablespoons of the beans onto each hash brown patty. Sprinkle each with about 2 tablespoons cheese. Top with 1 egg and sprinkle with an additional 2 tablespoons cheese. Pour the green sauce over and serve warm.

TIP: You can microwave the hash browns slightly before frying to reduce your cooking time. I use the frozen hash browns because of their ease, but you can also use four or five shredded russet potatoes for the hash browns.

GREEN SAUCE

—◆ ◆ ◆ ◆ ◆—

PREP TIME: 10 MINUTES
TOTAL TIME: 10 MINUTES
MAKES ABOUT 2 ½ CUPS

—◆ ◆ ◆ ◆ ◆—

6 tablespoons chicken broth

6 tablespoons all-purpose flour

½ cup diced yellow onion

2 (4-ounce) cans green chilies

2 tablespoons olive oil

1. Mix all the ingredients until smooth with a food processor or electric mixer.

2. Pour the mixture into a small saucepan and bring to a simmer over medium-low heat, stirring occasionally. Reduce the heat to low and cover, stirring occasionally, until you're ready to pour over the dish.

WASHING OFF THE DUST
(LUNCH, AKA DINNER)

ON MOST RANCHES, THE TIME BETWEEN BREAKFAST AND LUNCH (OR DINner as we call it in this part of the world) is when cowboys gather up cattle from a pasture and move them to a set of pens to be branded and vaccinated. On some outfits, a pasture may be as large as 10,000 acres, so coaxing the bovine beasts takes quite a bit of persistence and horse sense. Very few times during this procedure can I remember when it wasn't like the

Dust Bowl. When you take a patch of ground that is stomped clear of vegetation and then throw about three hundred cows and calves into the mix, it's dusty. So dusty that the crew will get enough dirt in their ears to grow a garden. The only things not covered in dust are their heads, as you can see when they take their hats off to wash up.

You can never be too sure when lunchtime will be, because an old cow doesn't wear a watch and she sure doesn't care if you're knee-deep in a mud hole and it's time for you to eat. But whether it's noon or well into the afternoon, those boys have worked up an appetite by the time they head back to camp.

Before they eat, it's time for a good rinsing. And sometimes there are just not enough stock tanks in the world to wash off all the dust, but they do their best. How much food they can shovel in usually depends on the time of year and if there is any more work that needs to be finished. Either way, the food will be hot and there will be plenty of it. Food is the best GPS of all—and they'll be straight back in no time for the next meal.

THE RECIPES

HEARTY HODGEPODGE SOUP

PREP TIME: 15 MINUTES

TOTAL TIME: 45 MINUTES

MAKES ABOUT 6 SERVINGS

1 pound ground beef

Salt and black pepper

1 yellow onion, chopped

2 (10.75-ounce) cans minestrone soup

1 (10-ounce) can Ro-Tel Diced Tomatoes & Green Chilies

1 (15-ounce) can Ranch Style Beans or Chili Beans

1 (15.5-ounce) can yellow hominy

1½ soup cans water

In my country, we call this type of dish a cupboard cleaner or a whatchucallit, made with whatever's left over. But it's guaranteed good—and you won't be able to call them off of it! Like an old hound chewing on a bone, they ain't quitting 'til it's either buried or gone. The blend of soup, beans, and hominy gives it a Southwest flavor, with canned tomatoes and chilies added for a little heat. It's a feel-good meal to fix on a cool fall day or when you're hearing sweet drops of rain hit the tin roof.

1. In a large skillet, brown the meat over medium-high heat. Season with salt and pepper to taste. When the meat is about halfway done, add the onion and continue cooking until the meat has completely browned and the onion is tender.

2. Drain the grease. Scrape the meat mixture into a soup pot.

3. Stir in the minestrone soup, Ro-Tel, beans, hominy, and water.

4. Cover and cook over high heat until it comes to a boil. Salt and pepper to taste. Reduce the heat and simmer for 30 minutes, stirring occasionally. Serve hot.

TIP: If Ranch Style Beans or Chili Beans aren't available at your store, you can make your own. Place a 16-ounce can pinto beans in a medium saucepan over medium-high heat. Stir in 2 teaspoons ketchup, ¼ teaspoon oregano, ¼ teaspoon cumin, and ¼ teaspoon chili powder. Bring to a boil, stirring occasionally. Reduce the heat to medium-low and simmer for 15 minutes, stirring occasionally.

SWEET-HEAT-BARBEQUE CHOPPED PORK SANDWICHES

The secret to good pork is slow cooking: the slower the better to make it tender. Often I cook pork in the smoker, but here is an easy indoor recipe. The barbeque sauce pulls this whole rodeo together.

PREP TIME: 5 MINUTES
TOTAL TIME: 2 HOURS
40 MINUTES
MAKES 5 OR 6 SERVINGS

Juice of 1 lime

2½ to 3 pounds pork loin

Seasoned salt and black pepper

Sweet Heat Barbeque Sauce
(*page 59*)

5 or 6 hamburger buns

Pickles, jalapeños, and sliced
onion for serving (*optional*)

SWEET HEAT BARBEQUE SAUCE

PREP TIME: 10 MINUTES

TOTAL TIME: 10 MINUTES

MAKES ABOUT 2 1/2 CUPS

1 cup ketchup

1 cup tomato sauce

1/4 cup light brown sugar

3 tablespoons Worcestershire sauce

2 tablespoons yellow mustard

2 tablespoons prepared horseradish

2 tablespoons apple cider vinegar

2 tablespoons hot sauce

1 tablespoon lime juice

2 teaspoons liquid smoke

1 teaspoon smoked paprika

1/4 to 1/2 teaspoon cayenne pepper

1. Preheat the oven to 325°F. Lightly butter an 8-x-11-inch casserole dish.

2. Pour the lime juice all over the pork and rub it in. Rub the pork with a generous amount of seasoned salt and pepper.

3. Place the pork in the baking dish and cover with foil. Bake for 2 hours, or until the internal temperature is about 150°F. Set aside to cool.

4. When the pork is cool enough to handle, place on a cutting board and chop into pieces.

5. Place the pork in a large saucepan and stir in the barbeque sauce. Simmer over medium-low heat for about 25 minutes, stirring occasionally.

6. Spoon the meat onto the hamburger buns. Serve warm with pickles, jalapeños, and sliced onion, if desired.

FOR THE SWEET HEAT BARBEQUE SAUCE

A sauce needs to blend well with its partner. Pork is always good with barbeque sauce, and this one carries a bit of sweet with its bite. You can also use this sauce with other meats and dishes.

1. In a medium saucepan, combine all the ingredients and whisk well.

2. Cook the sauce over medium-low heat for about 10 minutes, or until warmed through, stirring occasionally. The sauce can be served warm, at room temperature, or chilled.

CRISPY CHIPOTLE FAJITAS

PREP TIME: 25 MINUTES
TOTAL TIME: 55 MINUTES
MAKES 8 TO 10 FAJITAS

I stick butter, melted

I pound lean sirloin

I to 2 tablespoons olive oil

I medium yellow onion, sliced

Salt and black pepper

⅓ to ½ cup chopped chipotle peppers in adobo sauce

⅔ cup plum or raspberry jam

½ cup (4 ounces) cream cheese, softened

8 to 10 (6-inch) flour tortillas

Smoked pepper saddles up with plum jam and creates a savory sauce to pour over beef that will make your taste buds trot. I love the rich flavor of a tortilla crisped in butter. These crisp up just enough to get a little crunch with a whole lot of bite.

1. Preheat the oven to 350°F. Pour in enough butter to just coat an 8-x-11-inch baking pan.

2. Cut the beef into thin fajita strips.

3. Warm the olive oil in a 12-inch cast iron skillet over medium heat. Add the beef and onion. Season with salt and pepper to taste and cook, stirring occasionally, for about 10 minutes, or until the meat browns and the onion is tender. Drain the grease.

4. Stir in the chipotle peppers and adobo sauce, jam, and cream cheese. Feel free to add more of the adobo sauce for more heat. Cook over medium-low heat until warmed through, 8 to 10 minutes. It's OK if the cheese is not completely melted in.

5. Spread about 2 tablespoons of the meat mixture on each tortilla. Tightly roll the tortillas up and place crease side down in the baking pan. Pour half of the remaining butter over the top.

6. Bake for 15 minutes, then pour the remaining butter over the top of the tortillas. Continue baking for 10 to 15 minutes more, or until the tortillas are slightly browned on the top and crisp. Place on a wire rack and let cool just slightly before serving.

SLOPPY COWBOY JOES

PREP TIME: 25 MINUTES

TOTAL TIME: 25 MINUTES

MAKES 6 TO 8 SERVINGS

1½ pounds ground beef

1 yellow onion, diced

⅓ cup light brown sugar

1 (10-ounce) can **Ro-Tel Diced Tomatoes & Green Chilies,** drained

½ cup store-bought barbeque sauce or Sweet Heat Barbeque Sauce (*page 59*)

1 tablespoon yellow mustard

¾ to 1 cup shredded pepper jack cheese or your favorite shredded cheese

6 to 8 hamburger buns

I was visiting some folks when they said that we were going to have sloppy Joes for supper. I sure was excited because it's one of my favorite dishes. But I was highly offended when I walked into the kitchen and they poured it out of a can. You know me, I'm not against canned, but let's add in additional flavors that will still keep it simple with a homemade taste. A can of Ro-Tel for the spice, brown sugar for the sweet, and a kick of mustard, and you're on your way to a filling cowboy meal.

1. In a 12-inch cast iron skillet, cook the beef over medium-high heat until browned, about 10 minutes. Drain the grease.

2. Stir in the onion, brown sugar, Ro-Tel, barbeque sauce, and mustard. Reduce the heat to medium-low and simmer for about 10 minutes, stirring occasionally, until heated through and the flavors combine.

3. Slowly mix in the cheese and let cook for a few more minutes, until the cheese begins to melt.

4. Spoon the mixture onto the hamburger buns. Serve warm.

I've been so hungry that my stomach thought my throat had been cut and my belly was so empty it was rubbing blisters on my backbone.

THE MAP

◆ ◆ ◆ ◆

HAVE YOU EVER BEEN IN A NEW place or in a big pasture that you knew nothing about—one with no familiar landmarks? A pasture so big you couldn't see the other side of it in a day's ride?

When I was cooking for some folks about fifteen years ago near Dumas, Texas, I found myself in that situation. Although I followed the horses down to camp, I knew nothing about this ranch or the place where we were setting up. I mean, when it got dark, it was dark!

Well, I finally made it to camp. My alarm wasn't confused: It went off right on schedule at 3:45 A.M. My old stove, Bertha, did her job, and soon breakfast was underway. Some of the hands had come in that night, and I hadn't met them until the lantern at breakfast showed their faces. One old feller stuck out. He was bent but not quite broken, and I guessed his age at about 75 years young. He was just called Slim.

His face was tanned to leather, and he had been seasoned by time and weather, bowlegged by all the hours in the saddle, and he had a gait that was more a shuffle than a walk. He was a man of few words, but the few he did speak were full of wisdom passed down through ages of cowboy logic and lore. You could tell that the younger fellers all respected him by their demeanor when he was around. It was as if they were in the presence of a celebrity.

When the men had finished the vittles, just before they set off to do battle against cow and nature, they all dropped their dishes in the wreck pan and said, "Thank you, Cookie, it was sure good, and if we don't get run over this morning, we'll see you at noon." Slim, who was the last to rise from the table, a tad slower than the rest, dropped his plate and cup in and said, "Thanks, Cookie, for the meal; it was good, and you be careful today."

I watched him head down to the pens where they were roping out the morning mounts, a tradition that is still done on most outfits, and quite a sight to see. As if he had a sudden burst of energy and excitement about what was fixin' to take place, Slim's stride quickened. One of the other cowboys hollered out, "Sir, what are you riding today? I sure will rope him out for you." This gesture was an act of kindness and a sign of respect for a man who had done and seen his share from the saddle on the back of an old horse.

As the days passed along, Slim and I finally got a chance to visit. One evening after the supper dishes were all finished, he asked me, "Say there, Cookie, you still feel lost or are you about to get settled in the saddle?"

I told him that all I knew for sure was where the woodpile was and that the ball of fire still came up in the sky as it had for all those years.

"Do you need me to draw you a map of this place and point out the landmarks that make it what it is today?" From there, he took me on a journey through the places he had been. He drew me a map of trails and crossings of ranches and roads, and he outlined out a map of life:

When life gives you a string of horses, some will always be better than others, but don't give up on the bad ones too quick.

We all have to have a little extra riding at times to get settled in.

It takes a lot of wet saddle blankets to make a colt what you think he is supposed to be, just as it takes time to build a trusting, long-lasting relationship with a friend.

Always do your best and never ask another hand to do something you wouldn't do yourself.

Sometimes a shortcut across an old rough pasture may seem easier, but a feller can miss a lot of cows always taking the shortcut.

Never judge a man by what he rides or what he looks like. In time, that will figure itself out.

There are two things in life that matter most, your word and your work. Take care not to tarnish either one.

The short time I spent with Slim still echoes in my mind. I've come to realize that the wrinkles on his face were not just carved like sculpture but were a true map of the places he had been and the things he had seen. A map of hard times, but also of times I wished I had ridden through myself.

So if you are ever in need of a map or direction, remember that sometimes they are not written on paper but on faces and hearts. The direction in which we travel leads us down many trails, and the folks we meet can have a great impact on our journey and our life thereafter. I might have been a little turned around in my direction, but after a talk with Slim, I was no longer lost.

UPSIDE-DOWN PIZZA

PREP TIME: 25 MINUTES
TOTAL TIME: 50 MINUTES
MAKES 6 TO 8 SERVINGS

2 pounds ground beef

1 large yellow onion, chopped

1 (15-ounce) can tomato sauce

1 tablespoon minced garlic

1 (1.5-ounce) package spaghetti sauce mix

1 to 1½ cups sour cream

¾ cup shredded cheddar cheese

¾ cup shredded mozzarella cheese

Sourdough Pizza Crust (*page 69*), rolled out; or 1 (8-ounce) can crescent rolls, unrolled

2 to 3 tablespoons butter, melted

2 to 3 tablespoons grated Parmesan cheese

TIP: You can also use a store-bought pizza crust.

I usually don't make this right off the bat for a crew on a ranch because it's so good and I get tired of them asking, "When are you going to make that pizza deal again?" The recipe came by way of my Aunt Dortha. She is as good a cook as anybody I know, so if she sends a recipe, I think, "How fast can I make this?" It blends classic Italian sauce flavors with ground beef and cheese to create an easy, crowd-pleasing meal. If you don't have all the ingredients in your pantry, no matter what your means of transportation, whether it's horseback or horsepower, get to the store and get it done.

1. Preheat the oven to 350°F. Grease a 9-x-13-inch casserole dish.

2. In a 12-inch cast iron skillet, begin cooking the beef over medium heat. When it begins to brown, add the onion and continue cooking until the meat has completely browned. Spoon out the excess grease.

3. Reduce the heat to medium-low and stir in the tomato sauce, garlic, and spaghetti sauce mix. Let the mixture simmer for about 5 minutes to combine the flavors, stirring occasionally.

4. Scrape the mixture into the casserole dish. Spoon the sour cream onto the meat and spread out evenly. Sprinkle on the shredded cheeses.

5. Place the pizza dough or crescent rolls on top of the casserole. Brush with the melted butter and sprinkle with the Parmesan cheese.

6. Bake for about 25 minutes, or until the crust is golden brown. Serve hot.

SOURDOUGH PIZZA CRUST

PREP TIME: 15 MINUTES
TOTAL TIME: 35 MINUTES
MAKES ONE 14-INCH PIZZA
CRUST

3 cups Sourdough Starter
(*page 34*)

¼ cup olive oil

2 tablespoons sugar

2 teaspoons garlic salt

2 teaspoons baking powder

2 to 2½ cups all-purpose flour

Favorite toppings, such as
cheese, pepperoni, or sausage

TIP: Feel free to add your favorite Italian seasonings or Parmesan cheese to the dough to enhance the flavors of the crust.

When we were in a bind on a ranch and needed a crust for Upside-Down Pizza, Shannon and I came up with this recipe, which uses the sourdough starter that we always have on hand. We actually prefer it to any other crust. Try it with your next pizza or calzone or use with the Upside-Down Pizza (page 68).

1. Preheat the oven to 400°F. Lightly butter a large baking sheet.

2. In a large bowl, whisk together the sourdough starter, olive oil, sugar, garlic salt, and baking powder.

3. Slowly stir in enough flour to form a soft dough. Turn the dough out onto a floured surface. Lightly work the dough with the flour until all the stickiness is gone.

4. Roll the dough out to about ¼ inch thick. Top with your favorite toppings and bake for 15 to 20 minutes, or until the crust is golden brown.

Driving a good team of horses or mules is easy, but every once in a while, even they will get off the trail. If you lose focus, the road can get bumpy. But sometimes we have to hit a few bumps to wake up and pay attention to the road.

MEXICAN TORTILLA LASAGNA

PREP TIME: 25 MINUTES

TOTAL TIME: 55 MINUTES

MAKES 6 TO 8 SERVINGS

---

2 pounds ground beef

1 yellow onion, chopped

1 large jalapeño, diced

1 (1.25-ounce) package taco
seasoning

¾ cup water

1 (16-ounce) can refried beans

1½ (10-ounce) cans red
enchilada sauce

1 (10-ounce) can Ro-Tel Diced
Tomatoes & Green Chilies

8 to 10 large flour tortillas

1½ cups sour cream

3 cups shredded cheddar
cheese

There are two things that are always plentiful at the wagon in camp—full stomachs and tortillas. Tortillas are like gold, because they can be used for so many things. Let's load up the traditional Italian lasagna and flavor it like hearty enchiladas. The tortillas soften like noodles, absorbing the spicy flavors of the meat and sauce. When you set this out, be ready for a stampede.

1. Preheat the oven to 350°F. Lightly butter a 9-x-13-inch casserole dish.

2. In a 12-inch cast iron skillet, begin browning the meat over medium-high heat. When the meat begins to brown, add the onion and jalapeño. Continue cooking until the meat has browned completely and the onion is tender. Drain the excess grease.

3. Reduce the heat to medium-low. Stir in the taco seasoning and water. Simmer for 5 minutes, stirring occasionally.

4. While the meat is simmering, pour the beans into a small bowl and microwave for 1 minute, or warm in a small saucepan over low heat. Stir and set aside.

5. In a medium bowl, combine 1 can of the enchilada sauce with the Ro-Tel. Set aside.

6. Place a layer of tortillas on the bottom of the dish. You may need to rip them to make them fit evenly.

7. Spoon half of the beans onto the tortillas and spread evenly. Do the same with half of the sour cream.

8. Sprinkle half of the meat mixture over the top and then 1 cup of the cheese. Pour about half of the enchilada sauce/Ro-Tel mixture over the dish.

Around the wagon, every day is a holiday, and every meal a banquet.

9. Repeat steps 6 to 8.

10. Finish the dish by topping with one last layer of tortillas followed by the remaining 1 cup cheese and the remaining half can enchilada sauce. (You may not need to use all the tortillas.)

11. Bake for 30 minutes, or until bubbling around the edges. Serve hot.

GREEN PEPPER FRITO PIE

PREP TIME: 20 MINUTES
TOTAL TIME: 30 MINUTES
MAKES 6 TO 8 SERVINGS

2 pounds ground beef

1 yellow onion, chopped

1 large green bell pepper, chopped

1 cup diced tomatoes

3 tablespoons Worcestershire sauce

1 (15-ounce) can red enchilada sauce

Salt and black pepper

2 cups shredded cheddar cheese

2 to 3 cups Frito corn chips

Boy, this brings back childhood memories. At every rodeo or school game, the bestseller at the concession stand was Frito pie. Chili meat poured into a snack-sized sack of Frito chips was simple greatness. I thought I'd help this standby with a little more spice and give you more room to work with than just those little ole chip sacks. Dive in and feed the family, 'cause this is a classic.

1. Preheat the oven to 350°F.

2. In a 12-inch cast iron skillet (or other oven-safe skillet), begin browning the meat over medium heat. When the meat starts to brown, stir in the onion and green pepper. Continue cooking, stirring occasionally, until the meat has browned completely, about 10 minutes. Drain the grease.

3. Reduce the heat to medium-low and stir in the tomatoes, Worcestershire and enchilada sauces, and salt and pepper to taste. Simmer for 5 minutes, stirring occasionally.

4. Remove from the heat and sprinkle the cheese evenly over the meat mixture.

5. Place the skillet in the oven and bake for 5 to 10 minutes, or until the cheese melts.

6. Sprinkle the Fritos evenly over the top. Lightly press the Fritos into the pie and serve.

MEXICAN TRES-CORN BAKE

PREP TIME: 10 MINUTES

TOTAL TIME: 1 HOUR AND 10 MINUTES

MAKES 8 TO 10 SERVINGS

---

1 (8.5-ounce) box Jiffy Corn Muffin Mix

1 (15-ounce) can whole kernel corn, drained

1 (4.75-ounce) can or a heaping ½ cup creamed corn

½ cup diced yellow onion

¾ cup diced red bell pepper

1½ cups (about 7 ounces) chopped chorizo or spicy link sausage, cooked

1 cup sour cream

1 large egg, beaten

1 teaspoon salt

½ teaspoon black pepper

1 cup shredded pepper jack or cheddar cheese

If you think corn bread tastes dry and bland, then your food fantasy is about to come true! This three-corn creation offers a creamier and moister alternative to a plain side of corn or corn bread. There's one thing I always like with corn and that's meat. With some spicy sausage, this is a side dish that can stand on its own. Man, this is sounding better the more I think about it!

1. Preheat the oven to 350°F. Lightly butter an 8-x-11-inch baking pan or a 10-inch cast iron skillet.

2. In a large bowl, combine the Jiffy Mix, kernel corn, and creamed corn.

3. Stir in the onion, bell pepper, and sausage. Slowly stir in the sour cream, egg, and salt and pepper.

4. Pour half of the mixture into the pan. Sprinkle the cheese evenly over the top and then pour the remaining corn mixture over the cheese.

5. Bake for 50 to 60 minutes, or until the dish springs back slightly to the touch and just begins to brown around the edges. To retain the moisture, be careful not to overcook this dish. It will set up a bit more as it cools.

6. Remove from the oven and let cool for a few minutes. Serve warm or at room temperature.

Our country is so dry that when Noah's flood came, we only got a half inch!

CREAMY RICE BAKE WITH BLACK BEANS

PREP TIME: 20 MINUTES
TOTAL TIME: 45 MINUTES
MAKES 6 TO 8 SERVINGS

2 tablespoons butter

½ cup chopped yellow onion

½ cup chopped yellow bell pepper

½ cup chopped red bell pepper

½ cup chopped poblano pepper

2 cups cooked white rice (from 1 cup uncooked)

1 (15-ounce) can black beans, drained and rinsed

1 (10.5-ounce) can cream of celery soup concentrate

¼ cup milk

Like many of my recipes, this one came about while I was cooking on a ranch for five weeks. I always make a menu and a grocery list to cover all the meals while I'm out on the wagon, but sometimes it's hard to stick to the schedule. And when there isn't a Walmart for ninety miles and supplies are getting low, a good wagon cook learns to improvise. I have to work with whatever food I've got on hand. The black beans in this recipe are a nice change from the regular old pinto beans, which are a staple in a cowboy's diet. This dish is as colorful as it is flavorful and creamy.

1. Preheat the oven to 350° F. Grease an 8-x-11-inch casserole dish.

2. In a large skillet, melt the butter and cook the onion and peppers over medium heat, stirring, for about 10 minutes, or until tender. Remove from the heat.

3. In a large bowl, combine the pepper mixture with the rice and beans.

4. Stir the soup concentrate and milk into the rice mixture.

5. Scrape into the casserole dish and bake for about 25 minutes, or until the dish is hot. Serve warm.

TIP: This dish can be served warm, but stick it in the icebox overnight and it's a tasty chilled leftover.

SPICY BARBEQUE-AND-BACON BAKED BEANS

---◆ ◆ ◆ ◆---

PREP TIME: 15 MINUTES
TOTAL TIME: 40 MINUTES
MAKES 4 OR 5 SERVINGS

---◆ ◆ ◆ ◆---

5 slices thick-cut bacon, cut into 1-inch-wide pieces

1 (15-ounce) can Ranch Style Beans or Chili Beans, drained

1 (15-ounce) can pork and beans, drained

½ cup store-bought barbeque sauce or Sweet Heat Barbeque Sauce (*page 59*)

1 medium jalapeño, diced

1 yellow onion, chopped

¾ cup light brown sugar

4 teaspoons yellow mustard

I grew up on all sorts of beans as a kid. In fact, Mama told us kids they were a substitute for meat. Unfortunately, it's a common misunderstanding that canned beans can't be good. Sure, if you dump a can of baked beans on the table, they're going to taste canned. But if you take them and inject your own flavors, they can be resurrected. On Chopped: Grill Masters, *I even had judge Aarón Sánchez fooled with this recipe. The barbeque sauce brings sweetness, and the jalapeño provides a little of the heat.*

1. Preheat the oven to 350°F. Lightly grease an 8-inch square casserole dish.

2. In a medium skillet, cook the bacon over medium heat until three-quarters done. Drain and set aside.

3. In a large bowl, stir together both beans, the barbeque sauce, jalapeño, onion, brown sugar, and mustard.

4. Stir in the bacon, setting aside several pieces to be placed on top of the beans.

5. Scrape the mixture into the baking dish. Place the remaining bacon pieces on top.

6. Bake for 25 minutes, or until the beans are bubbling. Serve hot.

---◆ ◆ ◆---

TIP: If you don't have Ranch Style Beans or Chili Beans at your store, see the tip on page 56.

ONE-STOP BARBEQUE BEAN BAKE

PREP TIME: 20 MINUTES

TOTAL TIME: 60 MINUTES

MAKES 6 TO 8 SERVINGS

---

2 pounds ground beef

Salt and black pepper

2 medium yellow onions, chopped

1 to 2 jalapeños, diced

2 (15-ounce) cans pork and beans, drained

1 cup store-bought barbeque sauce or Sweet Heat Barbeque Sauce (page 59)

1 (7-ounce) can green chilies

1 (1.25-ounce) package chili seasoning

½ cup light brown sugar

½ cup ketchup

1 tablespoon yellow mustard

I've taken these baked beans to the next level to create a happy meal, kicked up a notch from one of my mom's recipes. It's a great dish for a crew, especially if they're working cows in cold conditions. Paired with a little corn bread or biscuits, it's all you need to fill up.

1. Preheat the oven to 350°F. Lightly butter a 9-x-13-inch casserole dish.

2. In a 12-inch cast iron skillet, begin browning the meat over medium-high heat. Season with salt and pepper to taste while cooking. When the meat is about halfway done, add the onions and jalapeños and continue cooking until the meat has fully browned and the onions are tender. Drain the excess grease.

3. Pour the mixture into the casserole dish and stir in the remaining ingredients. Taste the mixture, because you may want to add more barbecue sauce, brown sugar, ketchup, or mustard to suit your taste buds.

4. Bake for 30 to 40 minutes, or until the casserole is bubbling. Serve hot.

There are two things that make me more nervous than a long-tailed cat in a room full of rocking chairs: a Handyman Jack and a dry county.

RED "WHISTLE" BERRIES

PREP TIME: 5 MINUTES
TOTAL TIME: 2 HOURS AND
35 MINUTES
MAKES ABOUT 10 SERVINGS

1 pound dried pinto beans

1 large yellow onion, sliced

1 jalapeño, diced

1 ham hock (8 to 10 ounces)

1½ tablespoons dried cilantro

1 teaspoon seasoned salt

1 teaspoon garlic salt

1 teaspoon black pepper

Years ago, camp cooks gave this nickname to beans because they cause you to "whistle" after eating. I like beans to have a thick soup consistency, not watery. That's why, when cooking, you should add just enough water to keep them covered, which will create a thicker broth. That's the same reason I never soak beans unless I'm at a high elevation, where cooking can take longer. I use dried cilantro for a mellower flavor that doesn't overpower its partners. Pair this with Mexican Tres-Corn Bake (page 76) and you've got a full meal.

1. Pour the beans into a large soup pot. Pour enough water over the beans until they are covered by about 1 to 1½ inches.

2. Add the onion, jalapeño, ham hock, and cilantro. Cook over high heat until the mixture reaches a rolling boil, stirring occasionally.

3. Cover and boil hard for 30 minutes, stirring occasionally. As soon as the beans are boiling, you may need to add more warm water to keep them slightly covered throughout the cooking process.

4. Reduce the heat to medium. Stir in the spices. Cover and simmer for 1½ to 2 hours, stirring occasionally, until the beans soften. Season again to taste, if necessary, and serve warm.

TIP: You can use a 12-ounce package of salt pork instead of the ham hock. You folks at higher altitudes (over 3,000 feet) may find that it takes longer for beans to soften.

SMOKY MAC AND CHEESE

PREP TIME: 35 MINUTES
TOTAL TIME: 35 MINUTES
MAKES ABOUT 6 SERVINGS

---

3 cups dried large elbow macaroni

2½ cups milk

3½ to 4½ tablespoons all-purpose flour

6 slices (about 4 ounces) provolone cheese

4 ounces Velveeta cheese

3 tablespoons butter, cut into tablespoons

2 teaspoons Worcestershire sauce

1 teaspoon liquid smoke

1 teaspoon garlic salt

2 teaspoons lemon pepper

Salt and black pepper

My wife, Shannon, considers herself a connoisseur of macaroni and cheese. I don't know that word, but I think it's a fancy term for "expert." That clever woman gave it my favorite flavor without even building a fire. Provolone cheese and liquid smoke create a natural smoky flavor. The Velveeta gives a creaminess that every macaroni and cheese should have.

1. In a large pot of boiling salted water, cook the macaroni until tender. Drain and toss with a little butter or olive oil to prevent the noodles from sticking together. Cover and set aside.

2. In a 12-inch skillet, warm the milk over medium heat. Add 3½ tablespoons of the flour and stir for a few minutes until the milk thickens slightly and is smooth. Add the remaining 1 tablespoon flour, if needed, to thicken.

3. Tear the provolone into pieces and stir into the milk mixture until it melts. Cut the Velveeta into small pieces and add to the warm mixture. Add the butter. Continue stirring for a few more minutes until all the cheeses and the butter have thoroughly melted.

4. Reduce the heat to low and stir in the Worcestershire, liquid smoke, garlic salt, and lemon pepper.

5. Pour the cheese sauce over the noodles and stir well. Season with salt and pepper to taste. Serve hot.

THE LOOP

◆ ◆ ◆

WHEN I WAS ABOUT EIGHT YEARS old, Pa and I were going to gather cattle along the Red River. Before we started, Pa told me that we needed to go pick up some help, and I asked him if it was anybody I knew. "You haven't had the privilege of meeting Red Brown yet. He is a good man and a good cowboy."

We headed down a pasture road as the rising sun gave a hint of daylight and figures began to take shape. The cactus and mesquite added to the early morning canvas, and in the distance, I saw a dim light outlining an old barn. As we got closer, I could see a white mule and a feller standing beside him. He had on a pair of striped overalls and a conductor's cap. When we stopped and got out of the truck to help Red load up, I thought to myself, "This is an odd combination. I've never seen any cowboy riding a mule, and he sure isn't dressed like anyone I've seen in a branding pen." I whispered to my dad, "This is some strange help we picked up." He looked at me with one of those looks you never forget and said, "Young'un, you better mind your manners and pay close attention to that man. He will teach you a life's lesson today." Well, we loaded up and off we went to do cow battle. It was an easy gather, and we were quickly back at the branding pen.

As a young feller, my job was always running the hot branding iron back and forth from the fire. To my surprise, Red Brown and his old mule were the first to rope and drag. I thought to myself, "This is going to be a long day. They should have let someone else rope first."

After the first few loops he threw, I was shocked. Let me tell you, folks, this man could rope! He could throw from any direction and with both hands, and he never missed. I bet he could have even roped the ears off a jackrabbit. I was amazed at his skills and just hoped that some day I could rope like that.

We finished right after lunch and proceeded to load up and head home. On the ride home, I told Mr. Brown, "Sir, you sure can rope!" He just grinned, showing his big tobacco-stained teeth, and said, "I get lucky every now and then." And that was all he said. I sat there a little puzzled because if I could rope like that I would be telling everyone I knew and even telling some of them twice.

We turned at Red's gate, and he told my dad, "Mr. Rollins, just drop me off here. Me and that old mule will have a visit on the ride home." We let him out and started on our way home when Pa said, "I hope you learned something today." "Yep," I said,

"that feller don't talk much but he can sure rope." Pa looked at me for a moment and said, "Always remember that a gentleman lets his actions and his work do the talking and is not boastful about it. But most important, son, don't ever judge a man by what he rides or the hat on his head."

My dad and Red are both gone now, but I will never forget the many lessons they taught me just by the loops they threw. And even if their loops came up empty or short, which didn't happen often, what mattered was that they threw them.

MRS. O'DONNELL'S FRIED MEAT PIES

—— ◆ • ◆ • ◆ ——

PREP TIME: 35 MINUTES
TOTAL TIME: 45 MINUTES
MAKES 12 TO 15 (5-INCH) PIES

—— ◆ • ◆ • ◆ ——

1 pound ground beef

1 teaspoon smoked paprika

½ teaspoon ground cumin

½ teaspoon dried oregano

¼ teaspoon ancho chile powder

2 cups chopped cabbage

⅓ cup diced Anaheim peppers

⅓ cup diced jalapeño

⅓ cup grated carrot

⅓ cup chopped yellow onion

⅓ cup chopped green onions

2 teaspoons minced garlic

1 tablespoon Worcestershire sauce

2 to 3 tablespoons all-purpose flour

It didn't happen often for me in grade school, but once in a blue moon, I would pass the spelling test. That meant one thing—Mama would take me to the burger joint and get one of Mrs. O'Donnell's fried meat pies as a reward. I remember thinking that they were the best thing ever. If it hadn't been for Mrs. O, I might have never gotten out of the first grade. Well, I had to re-create her pies to pay tribute to our hometown cook. The ground beef mixture has just the right blend of Southern seasonings. Who knows, if Mrs. O hadn't gone out of business, her motivation may have made me a brain surgeon instead of a chuck wagon cook.

1. In a large cast iron skillet, brown the meat over medium heat. Add the paprika, cumin, oregano, and ancho chile and mix well.

2. Reduce the heat to medium-low and let simmer for about 3 minutes to blend the flavors.

3. Stir in the cabbage, Anaheim peppers, jalapeño, carrot, onion, green onions, and garlic. Reduce the heat to low, cover, and simmer, stirring occasionally, for about 5 minutes, or until the vegetables are tender.

4. Remove from the heat and stir in the Worcestershire. Add in just enough flour to absorb the grease.

5. Spoon about 2 heaping tablespoons onto each dough circle. Fold over and crimp the edges with your fingers or a fork.

6. In a medium saucepan, heat 2 to 3 inches of oil over medium-high heat until about 350°F.

7. Fry the pies, a few at a time, until golden brown, about 2 minutes per side. Serve warm.

Meat Pie Dough
(*recipe follows*)

Canola or peanut oil for frying

MEAT PIE DOUGH

PREP TIME: 10 MINUTES
TOTAL TIME: 10 MINUTES
MAKES 12 TO 15 (5-INCH) CIRCLES

2 ½ cups all-purpose flour

1 teaspoon baking powder

1 teaspoon salt

1 stick butter, chilled and cut into tablespoon-sized pieces

1 cup water

⅓ cup olive oil

> If Mrs. O hadn't gone out of business, I might have become a brain surgeon instead of a chuck wagon cook.

FOR THE MEAT PIE DOUGH

1. In a large bowl, combine the flour, baking powder, and salt.

2. Cut the butter into the flour with a fork or pastry cutter until it has a cracker-crumb consistency.

3. Slowly stir in the water until combined. Stir in the olive oil.

4. Flour your hands and knead the dough together for about 1 minute.

5. Turn the dough out onto a floured surface and knead, adding a bit more flour if necessary, until all the stickiness is gone. Roll out to about ⅛ inch thick. Cut into 5-inch circles (a Crisco shortening lid works well).

TATER SALAD WITH SWEET JALAPEÑO RELISH

PREP TIME: 35 MINUTES

TOTAL TIME: 2 HOURS AND 35 MINUTES

MAKES 6 TO 8 SERVINGS

---

7 or 8 red-skinned potatoes

⅔ cup diced pickled jalapeños

½ heaping cup diced red bell pepper

¼ cup sweet relish

4 teaspoons sugar

I yellow onion, chopped

½ cup chopped green onions

2 large eggs, hard-boiled

I cup mayonnaise, or to taste

2 teaspoons yellow mustard, or to taste

I teaspoon smoked paprika

Salt and black pepper

My wife, Shannon, and I were out cooking on a ranch and were looking for something different to go with hamburgers. I'm sure not one to turn away a fried tater, but when it's 105 degrees at noon, you know those boys would like something cool when they come in from branding. I boiled some potatoes and threw in a blend of jalapeño and relish for a sweet bite with just a hint of mustard and seasonings. Try to cut all the potatoes to roughly the same size so they cook evenly.

1. Cut the potatoes into 1- to 1½-inch pieces; you should have roughly 8 cups. Place them in a large pot and cover with cold water. Cook over high heat until boiling. Boil the potatoes for approximately 10 minutes, or just until tender. Be sure not to overboil them or they will become too mushy when you mix them with the other ingredients.

2. Drain the water off the potatoes and cover with cold water. Add a few ice cubes and set aside.

3. Meanwhile, in a small bowl, combine the jalapeños, bell pepper, relish, and sugar. Set aside.

4. When the potatoes have cooled, drain off all of the water. Mix in the yellow and green onions. Finely grate the boiled eggs over the potatoes and stir in.

5. Slowly begin mixing in the mayonnaise and mustard. Feel free to add a little more or less mayonnaise and mustard to your liking.

6. Stir in the jalapeño mixture and paprika. Season with salt and pepper to taste. You may want to adjust some of the flavors, such as more jalapeño or sweet relish.

7. Scrape the potato salad into a large bowl, cover, and chill in the icebox for at least 2 hours. Serve.

PIONEER BREAD

PREP TIME: 15 MINUTES
TOTAL TIME: 2 HOURS AND 15 MINUTES
MAKES 1 LOAF

1 (¼-ounce) package rapid-rise yeast

¾ cup warm water

⅓ cup cornmeal, plus additional for sprinkling

3 tablespoons sugar

2 teaspoons salt

1 large egg

3 tablespoons vegetable oil

2½ cups all-purpose flour

2 tablespoons butter, melted

The Dust Bowl was a hard time in history, especially for folks in my part of the country. My dad lived through that time, and he said this was the bread his mother would always fix. The cornmeal and butter on top give it a golden-brown crust.

1. Butter a 9-x-5-x-2-inch loaf pan.

2. In a large bowl, dissolve the yeast in the water.

3. Beat in the cornmeal, sugar, salt, egg, vegetable oil, and 1 cup of the flour for 2 minutes. Slowly stir in the remaining 1½ cups of flour.

4. Roll the dough out onto a floured surface and knead for about 2 minutes, until smooth and elastic.

5. Place the dough in a buttered bowl, cover with a tea towel, and let rise in a warm place for 40 minutes, or until nearly doubled in size.

6. Remove the dough from the bowl and lightly knead it down. Roll out to a roughly ¼-inch-thick rectangle. Fold one short side into the center and then the other, so the dough is folded into thirds, like a business letter. Roll the dough up starting from the short side and press down slightly. Place the loaf seam side down in the loaf pan. Brush with the melted butter and sprinkle with cornmeal.

7. Cover with a tea towel and let rise in a warm place for 50 minutes, or until nearly doubled in size.

8. While the bread is rising, preheat the oven to 375°F.

9. Bake for 25 to 30 minutes, or until golden brown. Let the bread cool slightly and turn out onto a towel or plate. Serve warm or at room temperature.

TWELVE DAYS DOWN THE TRAIL

◆ ◆ ◆

Man, it was an awesome sight,
To see twelve hundred Longhorns cross.
Horns and hooves a splashin',
In the evening's fading light.

Cowboys hooping and hollering,
Cattle and horses not wanting to go.
But here comes ole Cookie a cussin' and a
    whoopin',
Those old mules plodding along ever so slow.

Twelve days down the trail,
And we had finally crossed the Red.
Twelve days of dirt and wind,
And that young'un was ready to roll out
    his bed.

"Twelve days down the trail," he said,
"Seems like a year to me.
Now don't get me wrong, I'm glad I came
    along,
And look at all I've gotten to see."

'Bout that time we heard ole Cookie say,
"Button, don't you go to getting homesick.
Why you ain't worked long enough,
I don't even think you can draw no pay."

"Joe and Bill, ya'll got first watch,"
He heard the boss man say.
"The rest of you boys eat your grub and hit
    them rolls,
Tomorrow's going to be an awful long day."

Well, that night as he tried to sleep,
It wasn't like those eleven nights before.
All the hands were nervous and restless
And he couldn't even hear ole Hank snore.

He didn't know what time it was,
When the boss came riding in.
He said, "You boys get saddled and mounted,
There's a bad storm a comin' with lots of dirt
    and wind."

He was just fixin' to ride out of camp,
When he heard ole Cookie holler,
"Button, don't you get lost in that dirt
    storm.
And make sure you don't get bucked off ole
    Dollar."

Well, he reached into his pocket for a
    kerchief,
And around his face he drew it tight.
He rode out into total darkness
Full of dirt and black of night.

Darkened figures rode past him,
Like prairie ghosts in the wind.
Twelve days down the trail,
And the boy wished he was home again.

But he and ole Dollar had a job to do,
To head and turn all them steers around.
And there at the banks of the Red River,
He and ole Dollar stood their ground.

I know he never saw it coming,
That lead steer hit ole Dollar in the flank,
Knocking both horse and rider,
Down the steep, slick river's bank.

Well, the storm was finally over,
And the cattle had settled down.
We'd gathered back at the wagon,
Drinking coffee and just sittin' around.

That's when we noticed,
Ole Dollar came running back.
He was covered with dirt and mud.
But there was no rider in his kack.

In frantic desperation,
We started searching for that young
    lad,
Fearing the worst had happened,
But we hoped it might not be so bad.

Ole Hank was the first to find him,
And he let out a mournful cry,
"Boys, I've found him here in the sand,
But I fear he's about to die."

And before we could get to him,
The little lad was gone.
His arms reaching outward,
Pointing toward the direction of home.

So we wrapped him in a wagon sheet,
And dug a hole in that wet sand.
Twelve days down the trail,
Every man had a hat in his hand.

So if you ever cross this river,
A little marker you might find.
And burnt there in the wood
You will read these lines:

"Twelve days down the trail,
We laid him in the sand.
Twelve days down the trail,
This boy of twelve became a man."

ICEBOX BREAD

PREP TIME: 25 MINUTES
TOTAL TIME: 3 HOURS AND
45 MINUTES
MAKES 2 LOAVES

3½ to 4 cups all-purpose flour

2 (¼-ounce) packages
rapid-rise yeast

2 cups milk

¾ cup water

¼ cup vegetable oil

3 tablespoons sugar

1 teaspoon salt

4 cups whole wheat flour

TIP: It's a little tricky to
tell when this dough cooks
through because the top
tends to brown fast. If
possible, cook the breads in
a clear loaf pan so you can
see the bottom browning
and rotate the loaves halfway
through baking between the
top and bottom racks.

When you need a little extra time for the big meal tomorrow, mix the dough the night before and let it chill in the icebox. Mama loved this recipe because it makes two loaves, which is perfect for a big family. Or, you can freeze the second loaf for later.

1. Butter two 9-x-5-x-2-inch loaf pans, preferably Pyrex.

2. In a large bowl, combine 2½ cups of the all-purpose flour with the yeast. Set aside.

3. In a small saucepan, whisk together the milk, water, vegetable oil, sugar, and salt over medium-low heat until warm.

4. Add the warm milk mixture to the flour mixture and beat with a hand mixer for 3 minutes.

5. Gradually stir in the whole wheat flour with a spoon until combined. Slowly add enough of the remaining 1 to 1½ cups all-purpose flour to make a stiff dough.

6. Turn the dough out onto a lightly floured surface and knead for 5 minutes. Cover with a large bowl and let sit for 20 minutes.

7. Lightly knead the dough a few times and divide in half. Place the dough halves in the loaf pans, cover, and place in the icebox for 2 to 24 hours.

8. When ready to bake, remove the loaves from the icebox and let sit in a warm place for 20 minutes, or until nearly room temperature.

9. Meanwhile, preheat the oven 400°F with a rack on the bottom.

10. Bake for approximately 40 minutes, or until the loaves are golden brown and a toothpick inserted in the center comes out clean. Cool on a rack.

SQUASH BREAD

PREP TIME: 15 MINUTES
TOTAL TIME: 1 HOUR AND
5 MINUTES
MAKES 1 LOAF

1½ cups all-purpose flour

1 teaspoon baking powder

½ teaspoon baking soda

½ teaspoon salt

2 teaspoons cinnamon

¾ cup sugar

2 large eggs

½ cup vegetable oil

2 teaspoons vanilla extract

1⅓ cups grated yellow squash

TIP: You can also use zucchini in place of the yellow squash.

A garden planted with squash will multiply faster than penned-up rabbits. With a little dab of cinnamon and vanilla, you can transform regular yeller squash into a spiced bread. When I was growing up, we used to eat this harvest staple as a late afternoon snack after feeding cows or building fences. It can also double as a dessert and will sure help decrease your squash supply.

1. Preheat the oven to 350°F. Butter and lightly flour a 9-x-5-x-2-inch loaf pan.

2. In a large bowl, whisk together the flour, baking powder, baking soda, salt, and cinnamon. Set aside.

3. In a medium bowl, whisk together the sugar, eggs, oil, vanilla, and squash until combined.

4. Slowly whisk the egg mixture into the flour mixture just until moistened.

5. Pour the batter into the loaf pan. Bake for 45 to 50 minutes, or until a toothpick inserted in the center comes out clean.

6. Let the loaf cool slightly before turning the bread onto a towel or plate. Serve warm or at room temperature.

Squash in a garden will multiply faster than penned-up rabbits.

DILLY BREAD

PREP TIME: 30 MINUTES
TOTAL TIME: 2 HOURS AND 30 MINUTES
MAKES 1 LOAF

1 cup cottage cheese

¼ cup water

3 tablespoons butter, melted

2½ cups all-purpose flour

2 tablespoons sugar

1 tablespoon minced yellow onion

2 teaspoons dill seeds

1 teaspoon salt

¼ teaspoon baking soda

1 (¼-ounce) package rapid-rise yeast

1 large egg, beaten

You'll be sniffing out the scent of this bread like our beagle, Bonehead, on a fresh rabbit track. Dill seed tastes nothing like the dill-pickle taste you may be thinking of. The bread has a warm, savory flavor, with a hint of onion. Eat it fresh out of the oven, or let it cool and slice to give a sandwich a special flavor.

1. Butter a 9-x-5-x-2-inch loaf pan.

2. Stir the cottage cheese, water, and 1 tablespoon of the butter together in a medium saucepan over low heat until warmed. Set aside.

3. In a large bowl, combine 1½ cups of the flour, the sugar, onion, dill seeds, salt, baking soda, and yeast.

4. Slowly pour the cottage cheese mixture into the flour mixture. Add the egg and whisk until combined.

5. Stir in the remaining 1 cup flour until combined.

6. Cover the bowl with a tea towel and let rise in a warm place until nearly doubled in size, approximately 40 minutes.

7. Remove the towel and lightly knead the dough down. Place the dough in the loaf pan and cover with a buttered piece of wax paper. Let rise until doubled in size, about 40 minutes.

8. About 20 minutes before baking, preheat the oven to 350°F.

9. Remove the wax paper and bake for 30 to 40 minutes, or until the bread is golden brown and a toothpick inserted in the center comes out clean.

10. Let the loaf cool slightly before removing from the pan and brushing with the remaining 2 tablespoons melted butter. Serve warm or at room temperature.

THE LIFE OF A RANGE COW

DO YOU KNOW WHERE THAT STEAK ON YOUR PLATE originated? It sure didn't just walk up to the grocery store and slip into a cellophane wrapper. So let's go back to the beginning. Somewhere out there, often in harsh and desolate country, there is a cow—and not just any cow, but a range cow, who eats off the land.

In the cattle business, there is a large variance on how much range is needed for one cow. The more arid parts of the country are obviously limited in their grazing resources and can support fewer cows than areas with more grass. I've been on ranches that have had one cow to ten acres, one cow to one hundred acres, and even one cow to three hundred and twenty acres.

The cow is one of the hardest working four-legged beasts you'll find. She gave birth to your rib eye more than a year ago. She let her calf nurse for about two months before it began grazing on grass, while still relying on Mama's dairy factory. About six months later, it's time for weaning. At around four to five hundred pounds, the calf says, "Goodbye, Mama," and is placed in a separate pasture. Some ranchers sell the calves at this point or make the decision to let them graze to gain weight to seven to eight hundred pounds before selling them to a livestock auction, feedlot, or slaughtering house.

If this calf, often called a "yearling" at this stage, makes a trip to the feedlot, it will dine on a high-protein diet to gain weight and be sold. Now it's off to the processing plant, where it is graded on fat content and leanness. It is slaughtered and hung for two to four weeks in the cooler, depending on the buyer's preference, to age it and improve its flavor and tenderness. Then it's ready to be cut and wrapped into a variety of ground beef, rib eyes, brisket, and other cuts.

PRIMING THE PUMP
(APPETIZERS)

APPETIZERS SURE AREN'T TRADITIONAL chuck wagon fare, but I've been known from time to time to have a little something waiting for the boys when they got finished working the cows before supper. What's better than a cold beverage and something to graze on while you're waiting for the main show to take place?

Most of the meals I prepare are big enough that you're just looking for a recliner after, not a warm-up before. But it's like priming the pump; you've got to ease into supper slow sometimes before you open the floodgates.

I think the first time I was really introduced to an appetizer was in 1999 when I was entertaining at a museum event in Tulsa. These folks were duded up in their Sunday best, and I felt a little underdressed, being as all I had to pick from at the time was one dirty pair of Wranglers and one clean pair. There were fancy tablecloths, real china, and two too many glasses. And what was the deal with all those forks?

When it came time to sit down, a lady from Baltimore sat beside me. She leaned over and asked, "Don't you just love fine dining?" I told her I like any kind of dining as long as I didn't have to wash the dishes. Now, I had no clue they were planning on serving appetizers or even serve several courses. So when that waiter came by and put a small plate with three grilled shrimp, four crackers, and some sauce in front of me, I was worried. Either they didn't know serving sizes or they had some people show up who weren't invited. I didn't mind sharing, but we were going to have to stop at a truck stop on the way home and grab a couple of burritos, 'cause this wouldn't fill up a bird. I leaned over and whispered to that lady beside me, "These are awful small fixin's, ma'am, I guess they don't plan on anyone overeating tonight." She looked at me, grinned, and said, "You don't eat like this often, do you?" "No, Ma'am," I replied, "and I don't hope to any time soon if this is all they're going to give us!"

THE RECIPES

FIESTA CABBAGE SALSA WITH CITRUS SQUEEZE

PREP TIME: 15 MINUTES

TOTAL TIME: 6 HOURS AND 15 MINUTES

MAKES 9 TO 10 CUPS

1 (16-ounce) bag coleslaw

6 Roma tomatoes, chopped

2 medium purple onions, chopped

1 (12-ounce) jar diced pickled jalapeños, drained, juice reserved

3 tablespoons lime juice

Celery salt or garlic salt

When my wife, Shannon, first tried to get me to eat this, I thought, "I like salsa, but I'm not going to eat cabbage in no form or fashion!" You can cover an old ugly horse with a good saddle blanket, but he's still an old ugly horse under it all. But Shannon told me to at least saddle it before I got bucked off. Well, folks, she was right, as always, and I'm a believer. This is a fresh, crisp salsa—a great grazing food to serve with chips, and I also put it on tacos or any Mexican dish.

1. In a large bowl, mix the coleslaw, tomatoes, and onions together.

2. Begin by adding ½ cup diced jalapeños to the mixture. This is a judgment call; depending on how hot you like your salsa. I like more of a bite, so I typically add about ¾ cup jalapeños. Toss in about ¼ cup of the jalapeño juice (again, a judgment call, I usually add a little more). Add the lime juice and celery or garlic salt to taste.

3. Cover and place in the icebox for about 6 hours or overnight to let the flavors mingle. The longer it sits, the juicier it gets.

Good friends are like good saddles; the more time you spend with both, the better you feel.

CORN SALSA

PREP TIME: 10 MINUTES
TOTAL TIME: 2 HOURS AND
10 MINUTES
MAKES ABOUT 6 CUPS

---

1 (15.8-ounce) can black-eyed
peas, drained

1 (10-ounce) can Ro-Tel Diced
Tomatoes & Green Chilies,
drained

1 (15.25-ounce) can whole
kernel corn, drained

¼ cup balsamic vinegar

2 teaspoons lime juice

1 cup diced purple onion

2 Anaheim peppers, diced

1 jalapeño, diced

1 avocado, halved, pitted,
peeled, and diced

Salt and black pepper

Chips for serving

I do love salsa, especially if it's fresh and cold. This mixture is a garden party with black-eyed peas, corn, and avocado. It's one of those toss-and-go dishes that requires no effort. I'll load up a chip, taco, or even a salad with this concoction.

1. In a large bowl, combine all the ingredients except the salt and pepper and chips.

2. Cover and chill for 2 hours. Season with salt and pepper to taste. Serve with chips.

TIP: Sometimes our little store doesn't carry Anaheim peppers, and I've substituted 4 or 5 pickled pepperoncinis. You can also use black beans instead of the black-eyed peas.

GREEN CHILE CHIPOTLE RELISH WITH CREAM CHEESE

PREP TIME: 15 MINUTES

TOTAL TIME: 1 HOUR AND 15 MINUTES

MAKES 6 TO 8 SERVINGS

Green Chile–Chipotle Relish
(*page 148*)

1 (8-ounce) block cream cheese, softened

Crackers for serving

The heat from the relish blends well with the coolness of cream cheese and will make your partygoers give you an "attaboy!"

1. After removing the chipotle relish from the heat, scrape the mixture into a small bowl, cover, and place in the icebox for 1 hour, or until chilled.

2. Pour the relish over the block of cream cheese and serve with crackers.

Life, like a bucking horse, is going to buck you off at times. Just remember to get back on and finish.

RED RIVER SMOKY CHIP DIP

PREP TIME: 8 MINUTES
TOTAL TIME: 1 HOUR AND
8 MINUTES
MAKES ABOUT 2 CUPS

---

1 small jalapeño

1 cup sour cream

1 (8-ounce) block cream cheese

1 tablespoon Worcestershire
sauce

1 teaspoon liquid smoke

1 teaspoon smoked paprika

⅛ to ¼ teaspoon ancho
chile powder

Chips for serving

This recipe has certain ingredients that I always go to because they are the best in everything: smoky, hot, and creamy. It's a quick dip that blends up fast for a great complement to a chip. I've also spread it on a sandwich for a change from plain old mayonnaise.

1. Remove the seeds from the jalapeño (unless you like the bite) and place in a food processor.

2. Add the sour cream, cream cheese, Worcestershire, liquid smoke, paprika, and chile powder. Blend together for about 1 minute, or until smooth.

3. Cover and chill for 1 hour. Serve with chips.

An old-timer once told me, "Making good horses is like making a good life and a good name for yourself. It takes a lot of miles and wet saddle blankets."

UNWANTED GUESTS

IT WAS MAY ON THE SILVERBROOK Ranch near Abilene, Texas, during two weeks of spring works. I was cooking for a crew I had never met, in country I had never been in, using their wagon instead of mine. Now, that might sound like a challenge, but I like an opportunity to overcome circumstances that I can't control nor predict. I

I'm talking skeeters so big they could carry off a laying hen.

should have known it was going to be a long two weeks when mounted cowboys came dragging in two old knot-headed mules to harness to the wagon. They were probably the most rank and stubborn team I've ever had to work with, and did I mention that we were going to move camp every day after lunch? I never even had time to set up the fly.

Spring works in May in that part of Texas can be muggy, to say the least. It just so happened at this particular time there had been a lot of rain, and that made for a bumper crop of mosquitos, chiggers, and ticks. I'm talking skeeters so big they could carry off a laying hen, ticks that were half the size of snapping turtles, along with fire ants and the occasional rattlesnake. What a good mixture! Was this the plague they talked about in the Bible, a pestilence of

great magnitude? But I took the reins and pulled back hard and remembered that this is normal ranch cooking in the spring in my part of the world.

It was too hot to set up a teepee so everyone just threw out their bedrolls on the ground. This actually turned out to be the only upside because the skeeters couldn't make up their minds which target looked the best. The buzzing got so bad I thought I was sleeping on the tarmac at Dallas/Fort Worth. Somebody call Air Traffic Control and let's see about closing this landing strip down, I'm getting low on blood supply!

After several days, time and exhaustion finally took over and I was able to sleep through anything nibbling on me. I was beginning to look like a man with a case of chicken pox on steroids. You know that bug spray called "OFF!"? Well, I'm here to testify you can't put enough ON to turn them OFF! I used it everywhere, even gargled with it, but to no avail. These skeeters were immune to chemical warfare. I needed a flamethrower, or maybe I should've slept under a washtub like a turtle hiding from a raccoon.

Every morning, under the early cloak of darkness, it was hard to see all the damage, but by noon you could sure tell. The whole crew looked like they had hives—or any other scratching disorder known to man or beast. I had tried different home remedies passed down from one wagon cook to another. From rubbing garlic or ash all over our bodies to being smoked by the fire, but nothing worked. This battle had been well planned by the skeeters, and they were on their way to victory. The only saving grace was that there were only two more days and one agonizing night on the skeeters' buffet line. In fact, I think those skeeters paid the fireflies to spell out a flashing sign, "All You Can Eat," right over our camp.

At the end of those two weeks, I had never been so glad for a spring works to end. The crew was great, and they told me the food was the best ever, but I couldn't even begin to grill enough steaks for them to fight the anemia and low blood pressure. We all looked like a colony of lepers when we got back to headquarters. I loaded my stuff in my old Ford pickup and sped out of there as fast as I could, hoping the skeeters wouldn't follow.

PICKLED OKRA AND JALAPEÑO CHEESE DIP

PREP TIME: 10 MINUTES
TOTAL TIME: 40 MINUTES
MAKES 6 TO 8 SERVINGS

---

1 (8-ounce) block cream cheese, softened

½ cup sour cream

½ cup diced pickled okra

¼ to ⅓ cup diced pickled jalapeños

1 tablespoon Worcestershire sauce

½ teaspoon garlic powder

½ teaspoon smoked paprika

¼ teaspoon red pepper flakes

¾ cup crushed Ritz crackers

2 tablespoons butter, melted

Crackers or chips, for serving

In my country, there's always a lot of okra, especially during harvest time, and you have to get creative trying to get rid of it all. I love pickled okra, and mixed with jalapeños and cream cheese, this is simple comfort food. The Ritz cracker crust makes a buttery crunchy topping.

1. Preheat the oven to 325°F. Lightly butter a pie pan, round cake pan, or 10-inch cast iron skillet.

2. In a medium bowl, beat together the cream cheese and sour cream until smooth. Lightly beat in the okra, jalapeños, Worcestershire, garlic powder, paprika, and red pepper.

3. Scrape the mixture into the pan or skillet.

4. In a small bowl, combine the crushed crackers and butter. Sprinkle over the cream cheese mixture, pushing in slightly.

5. Bake for about 30 minutes, or until warmed through. Serve warm with crackers or chips.

CHEESE CRISPS

PREP TIME: 5 MINUTES
TOTAL TIME: 15 MINUTES
MAKES 20 TO 25 CRISPS

1 cup shredded sharp cheddar cheese

½ cup grated Parmesan cheese

½ (4-ounce) can green chilies

Hot sauce (optional)

This recipe came about by accident. You know when you bake a cheesy dish and a little of it falls over the side and onto the baking sheet below? It hardens, and I like to scrape it up and eat it. Well, this recipe gets right to the heart of the matter with tangy sharp cheddar, Parmesan, and a little kick. Just be sure to use parchment paper so these fellers pop right off and into your mouth.

1. Preheat the oven to 350°F. Place a piece of parchment paper on a baking or cookie sheet.

2. In a medium bowl, combine the cheddar and Parmesan cheeses. Slowly toss in the green chilies so they don't clump up.

3. Scoop a heaping teaspoonful of the cheese mixture and drop onto the paper. Lightly pat down the center. Repeat using the remaining cheese. Add a drop or two of hot sauce, if desired.

4. Bake for 8 to 10 minutes, or until the outside edges become dark brown. You can err on the side of cooking the crisps a little longer, because they will become crispier.

5. Remove the paper from the pan and place on a cool countertop. Allow to cool before removing the crisps from the paper. Serve.

It hasn't rained here in so long it's drier than a popcorn fart in a whirlwind.

COWBOY SUSHI

PREP TIME: 20 MINUTES

TOTAL TIME: I HOUR AND
30 MINUTES

MAKES 3 ROLLS; 18 TO 22 PIECES

3 (5- to 8-ounce) sirloin steaks
or thin-cut Milanesa

Lime juice

Meat tenderizer

Seasoned salt

Black pepper

⅓ cup cream cheese, softened

I to 2 jalapeños, cut into thin
2-inch-long spears

⅓ medium-sized cucumber, cut
into thin 2-inch-long spears

2 green onions, chopped

Cowboy Sushi Sauce
(*recipe follows*)

I avocado, halved, pitted,
peeled, and thinly sliced

Lemon juice (*optional*)

Hold the horses, 'cause this is an unlikely pair. Ever since Shannon got me hooked on sushi, it's been one of my favorites, but I wanted to make it cowboy style. Using thin steaks instead of rice beefs up the protein in my sushi. The fresh flavors of cucumber and avocado bring out the more traditional side of sushi. Tanoshimu—enjoy!

1. Unless you are using the Milanesa, wrap the sirloin steaks with plastic wrap and flatten with a meat hammer until about ⅛ inch thick, or as thin as possible and into approximately three 6-x-11-inch rectangles.

2. Remove the plastic and rub both sides of each piece with several drops of lime juice. Repeat with a few shakes of the meat tenderizer and seasonings. Cover and let sit for 30 minutes in the icebox.

3. Preheat a grill to low.

4. Remove the meat from the icebox and let warm to room temperature before grilling. Grill the meat over low heat for 2 to 3 minutes per side, until rare to medium-rare. You can also pan-fry the steaks by searing them on both sides over high heat in a cast iron skillet. Just be sure to keep the meat on the rare to medium-rare side because it will be easier to handle and more tender. Cool to room temperature.

5. Spread a thin layer of the cream cheese evenly over one side of each steak. Place about a 1½-inch-wide row of jalapeño and cucumber spears closer to one long side of the steaks, using your judgment about how much to include.

6. Sprinkle the green onions on top. Drizzle about 1 tablespoon of the sushi sauce on top of the vegetables.

TIP: The trick to this dish is having a thin cut of meat. Oftentimes I can find thin-cut Milanesa, which is beef top round cut extra thin; it works great here. You can also have your butcher cut an extra-thin piece of top round or sirloin so you don't have to pound your own meat.

7. Starting with the long side with the vegetables, tightly roll up the steak. Cover and place in the icebox for 10 minutes.

8. Cut the rolls into ¾-inch-thick pieces. Top the rolls with the avocado slices. You can squeeze a little lemon juice over the avocado to keep it from browning. Drizzle with the sushi sauce or use for dipping and serve.

COWBOY SUSHI SAUCE

PREP TIME: 5 MINUTES
TOTAL TIME: 5 MINUTES
MAKES ABOUT ¾ CUP

¼ cup plus 1 tablespoon
mayonnaise

1¼ tablespoons prepared
horseradish

1 tablespoon Worcestershire
sauce

1¼ teaspoons soy sauce

1 teaspoon lime juice

1 teaspoon liquid smoke

2 teaspoons light brown sugar

When I eat sushi, one of the best things is the sauce that is drizzled over it. This sauce enhances the Cowboy Sushi with a smoky Asian flavor. It's great for drizzling or dipping.

In a small bowl, whisk together all the ingredients until smooth. Serve with the sushi rolls.

BITE-SIZED BJTS

PREP TIME: 15 MINUTES
TOTAL TIME: 30 MINUTES
MAKES 8 SERVINGS

4 slices thick-cut peppered bacon, cut in half

½ stick butter, softened

8 slices French bread

1 large tomato, thinly sliced

8 slices queso fresco or fresh mozzarella

1 large jalapeño, cut into small spears

TIP: If you can't find peppered bacon, you can rub coarse-ground black pepper onto uncooked thick-cut bacon, slightly pushing it in.

Who doesn't love a BLT? But let's make it a little smaller, for a warm-up to the main course. A little jalapeño takes the place of the lettuce. Served open-faced, the peppered bacon is the only seasoning you'll need for this easy appetizer.

1. Preheat the oven to 425°F.

2. In a medium cast iron skillet, cook the bacon over medium heat until browned.

3. Butter the bread slices on both sides. Place the bread on a baking sheet. Top each slice with 1 or 2 slices of tomato, 1 piece of bacon, 1 slice of cheese, and 2 or 3 jalapeño spears.

4. Bake for 10 to 15 minutes, or until the bread is lightly toasted and the cheese has melted. Serve warm.

APRICOT GRILLED CHEESE

PREP TIME: 20 MINUTES
TOTAL TIME: 20 MINUTES
MAKES 10 TO 12 SERVINGS

1 stick butter

1 (15-ounce) can apricot halves, drained

½ cup light brown sugar, plus more for sprinkling (*optional*)

10 to 12 slices cheddar cheese, cut into 2-inch squares

10 to 12 slices French bread, ¾ to 1 inch thick

I know what you're thinking: "Kent has lost his mind!" But if you like grilled cheese, give this a try because it will probably surprise you as much as it did my wife when I first put it together. Sometimes you have to think outside the box. I was looking through the pantry one day and saw a can of apricots sitting there. I knew apricots and brown sugar caramelize together, but I wanted something tangy and salty to pair with them, which is when I added the cheddar cheese.

1. Melt ½ stick of the butter in a large cast iron skillet over medium heat.

2. Roll both sides of the apricot halves in the brown sugar until coated. Add the apricots to the skillet, pitted side down. Cook for 2 to 3 minutes, or until slightly softened, and flip.

3. Place 1 slice of cheese on each apricot. Spoon the butter mixture from the skillet over the apricots. Keep spooning until the cheese melts. Remove the apricots from the skillet. Set aside.

4. Melt the remaining ½ stick butter in the skillet. Add the bread slices and sop both sides with the butter. Toast on both sides until golden brown. Remove from the skillet.

5. Top the bread with the apricots. Lightly sprinkle with brown sugar, if desired, and serve warm.

AVOCADOS ON THE HALF SHELL

PREP TIME: 20 MINUTES
TOTAL TIME: 30 MINUTES
MAKES 8 SERVINGS

½ pound ground beef

½ teaspoon ground cumin

Salt and black pepper

2 medium jalapeños, finely diced

2 green onions, finely diced

2 teaspoons Worcestershire sauce

4 avocados, halved and pitted (leave the skin on)

Juice of 1 lime

Coarse sea salt

½ to 1 cup shredded pepper jack cheese

They don't grow too many oysters where I come from. Usually the only things running around here on the half shell are armadillos. But armadillos are hard to clean, so the easier alternative is avocados, which come with their own built-in bowl. Fill up those suckers with some spicy meat and cheese, and you don't have to take a trip to the coast. You can also serve two halves per person and make this a main course.

1. Preheat the oven to 400°F.

2. In a medium cast iron skillet, begin browning the beef over medium heat. Stir in the cumin. Season with salt and pepper to taste. When the beef has begun to brown, add the jalapeños and green onions. Continue cooking for about 8 minutes, or until the beef has cooked through.

3. Remove from the heat. Stir in the Worcestershire.

4. Lightly sprinkle the avocados with the lime juice and sea salt. With a slotted spoon, evenly scoop the beef mixture into the pitted centers of the avocados. Sprinkle the tops with cheese.

5. Place the avocados on a baking sheet and bake for 5 to 10 minutes, or until the cheese melts. Serve warm.

Usually the only things running around here on the half shell are armadillos.

COWBOY CURES

I'VE NEVER SEEN A PHARMACY close to camp when we were out on the wagon, so a feller better be stocked with some cure-alls. These homemade remedies have been passed down by generations of old-timers and wagon cooks.

ARTHRITIS An old cowboy named Mack asked me if I had any honey on the wagon. He told me, "I put a teaspoon in my coffee every morning because it helps my arthritis and aching bones."

BROKEN TOOTH I was in southwestern New Mexico for about three and a half weeks when a feller got a kick in the mouth by a calf that broke his tooth in two. Now I'm just warning you, the American Dental Association doesn't approve of this, but I took a little J-B Weld and with two green sticks, I sealed that tooth. When he finally made it back to town, the dentist wasn't very happy, but he did say it was a pretty clever fix in a tight spot.

CHAFING It's pretty common for a cowboy to get chafed in places he doesn't want to talk about. Cornstarch will dry it up better than baby powder and is always readily available on the wagon.

COLD SORE The tart chemical powdered alum will help dry up a cold sore. Not rec-ommended for people who already have a sour disposition.

COUGH/CONGESTION Grind wild sage and rub onto the chest or throat before bed-time. Cover with a warm rag for a menthol effect to ease the cough and/or congestion. Just don't get the plant confused with cooking sage, or you'll be mistaken for a Thanksgiving turkey.

CUTS AND SCRATCHES An old cowboy had a cut on his arm from running into a barbed wire fence. He broke a cactus pad in half and rubbed the juice on his arm. Like aloe, the juice helps the healing process. If you get bucked off in a cactus patch, call it acupuncture.

EARACHE Place a few drops of warm sweet olive or almond oil in the ear to ease an earache.

HEMORRHOIDS Now I know many of you don't have a problem with hemorrhoids, but when you spend twelve hours a day in the saddle, they can become a problem. Pour a few drops of kerosene or coal oil on a piece of gauze and rub on your hemorrhoids. Just be careful not to back up to the fire.

INSECT BITES Mix a little meat tenderizer with water to make a paste. Rub onto insect bites and cover with a Band-Aid to ease the sting and/or itching. It will also help pull the poison out. I've also used chewing tobacco.

SINUS RELIEF A garlic clove is nature's best antibiotic. Eating a clove a day will ward off everything from vampires to a sinus infection.

SORE THROAT Place a few drops of camphor on a lump of sugar and allow it to dissolve in the mouth to ease a sore throat. Or fill a coffee cup about one third with whiskey. Add a teaspoon of lemon juice and a tablespoon of honey and fill the rest with hot coffee and drink up. I have known some fellers who pretended to cough just to have another magic elixir.

SPIDER BITE I've been bit, poked, and punched by more things than I can count. For a spider bite, tape a penny to it. Be sure that old Abe's head is facing down so he can see what he's up against. The copper in the penny will draw the poison out. The older the penny, the better.

STOMACHACHE Take a few drops of peppermint oil to ease a stomach pain or help with digestion.

SUNBURN A tablespoon of apple cider vinegar a day will help with overall good health. Any type of vinegar is also good for taking the sting away when rubbed on a sunburn. The juice from a cactus pad will also alleviate the discomfort.

TOOTHACHE Strike a match and let the tip burn off. Crumble the match tip and one aspirin onto a small piece of paper bag and add a couple drops of whiskey. Ball it up and pack it on the tooth. The burnt sulphur from the match helps to seal the tooth, and the whiskey fights infection and eases pain.

PUT ON YOUR SHUT-UP DOGS
(SUPPER)

WHEN THE WORK IS FINISHED AND THE DAY IS GETTING CLOSE TO SUPPER, everyone's feet are usually aching. Those boys are looking for something comfortable to put on, and the first things they grab are those shut-up dogs. You've probably heard the old saying "My dogs are barking!" Let's quiet those hounds with some comfortable shoes.

Cowboy boots are made for riding, so when those boys get the chance, they put on something that is lighter and softer. Now I've seen all types of shut-up dogs, from tennis shoes to moccasins, but I don't think I have ever seen a cowboy wear a pair of flip-flops around the wagon because everything in camp will poke you, bite you, or burn you.

Things will get better now 'cause when your feet are happy, the rest of you will soon follow. Now's the time when those fellers gather around the wagon. This is the best time of the day for them, because they can unwind, relax, and let it all go. Laughter is prevalent, along with a healthy dose of B.S. It wouldn't be a good cowboy story if the truth wasn't stretched tight every once in awhile.

There is a great deal of respect, as well as admiration, that goes on around camp with a good crew. No one is left out, and the whole gang gathers under the fly of my old wagon. It's a ritual we look forward to every evening. Just as they anticipate supper, I love to hear the stories, laughter, and sometimes even a little wisdom. The camaraderie goes on until I finish supper, and then I tell those boys, "Let's eat it before it gets cold." There's always plenty of food and one biscuit left in the Dutch oven because a true cowboy will never take the last of anything.

I like to make folks feel like they're at home at the wagon, because when you're out for weeks at a time, it's good to be comfortable. And when my guests are comfortable in their surroundings, the more likely they are to eat everything on the plate, which makes my cleanup easier.

So whether you're out on the range or in the comfort of your own home, dig in that closet and find something to silence those hounds, 'cause it's suppertime!

THE RECIPES

---◆·◆·◆---

BUTTER-AND-BACON-BAKED CORNISH GAME HENS

PREP TIME: 10 MINUTES
TOTAL TIME: 1 HOUR 40 MINUTES
MAKES 4 TO 6 SERVINGS

2½ cups chicken broth

1 (10.75-ounce) can cream of chicken soup concentrate

4 Cornish game hens

Olive oil for coating

¼ cup seasoned salt

¼ cup lemon pepper

1 teaspoon garlic salt

1 teaspoon dried sage

2½ sticks butter

8 slices thick-cut bacon or peppered bacon (see *Tip*, page 119)

Growing up, we raised and processed chickens, so I have a few tricks up my sleeve for getting rid of a yard bird. When I first saw game hens, though, I thought someone must have picked them a little too early. They are a tender little bird when cooked right. Cover them with a little broth, bacon, and butter, and they'll cook up fork-tender and juicy.

1. Preheat the oven to 325°F.

2. In a large bowl, whisk together the chicken broth and soup concentrate until smooth. Pour the mixture into a large casserole dish or deep 12-inch Dutch oven. Set aside.

3. Coat each hen generously with the olive oil.

4. In a small bowl, combine the seasoned salt, lemon pepper, garlic salt, and sage. Rub the seasonings over the hens, reserving about 4 teaspoons.

5. Place ½ stick of the butter in each hen's cavity. Cut the remaining ½ stick of butter into small chunks and place in the casserole dish.

6. Lay the hens in the dish or Dutch oven, breast sides up. Cross 2 slices of bacon on each hen. Sprinkle the remaining 4 teaspoons seasoning over the tops.

7. Cover with tin foil or the Dutch oven lid and bake for 1½ hours, or until the internal temperature is about 165°F and the hens are cooked through. Be sure to baste them at least twice with the broth while cooking. About 5 minutes before the hens have finished cooking, remove the foil and let brown. Baste once more before serving.

SUNDAY HEN AND SOURDOUGH DUMPLINGS

Chicken and dumplings is one of those true Southern comfort foods. Mama made it most Sunday nights. I've made dumplings out of canned biscuits, tortillas, and piecrust—nearly anything you can imagine. But sourdough dumplings give a different tang that goes well with chicken. When this cooks, it creates a thick, creamy broth.

PREP TIME: 50 MINUTES
TOTAL TIME: 50 MINUTES
MAKES 6 TO 8 SERVINGS

7 cups water

2 teaspoons salt, plus more to taste

4 boneless chicken breasts

1 pint half-and-half

½ stick butter

1½ cups Sourdough Starter (page 34)

1½ tablespoons sugar

½ tablespoon baking powder

2 tablespoons vegetable oil

1½ cups all-purpose flour

2 tablespoons cornstarch

Black pepper

1. Combine 6 cups of the water with 1 teaspoon of the salt in a large saucepan. Add the chicken and cover. Bring to a boil over high heat. Reduce the heat to medium and cook until tender, 15 to 20 minutes. Remove the chicken and set aside to cool. Reserve the cooking liquid.

2. Add the half-and-half and butter to the chicken broth. Cook over medium heat until it begins to simmer, stirring occasionally.

3. Meanwhile, slice the chicken into bite-sized pieces. Add the chicken pieces to the broth and continue simmering for 20 minutes, stirring occasionally.

4. Meanwhile, whisk together the starter, sugar, remaining 1 teaspoon salt, baking powder, and oil in a large bowl. Slowly stir in the flour to form a soft dough.

5. Pinch off about 1-tablespoon-sized pieces of the dough and add to the broth. Repeat until the dough is gone.

6. Let the dumplings cook for 5 minutes, stirring occasionally.

7. Dissolve the cornstarch in the remaining 1 cup warm water in a small bowl and add to the broth. Continue cooking for 5 to 10 minutes, or until the mixture thickens, stirring constantly. Season with salt and pepper to taste. Serve hot.

NOT JUST ANY KITCHEN TABLE

WE ALL HAVE THEM, AND THEY come in an assortment of sizes and as many different styles and colors as you can imagine. I remember our first one. It was green and gold with padded chairs and metal legs that shone like a silver dollar. We were in tall cotton, as Pa would say.

At mealtime, my mother made sure that we all gathered around the table and remembered our manners. She was a good cook, and when you're eating with a family of six, you better dig in quick 'cause if you don't, you might not get any. We didn't have a lot, but I can't ever remember going hungry.

My sister, Cindy, who has cerebral palsy, was the last at the table, especially in her younger years before she got a motorized wheelchair. Most times Dale, Randy, or I might push her into the kitchen. Pa sat down, and the meal would commence. It never failed that someone would spill a glass of iced tea, usually Randy. Then came the familiar speech by Mama about how she wished we could get through one meal without someone making a mess. It was also not uncommon for one of us, generally Dale or me, to slip something under the table to our dependable plate cleaner—the dalmatian dog, Trey. We were all supposed to clean our plates before leaving the table, which was often difficult when Mama was serving something green. But we had figured out, with the help of our older brother, Randy, that you could wrap any vegetable in a piece of bread and ole Trey would swallow it in one gulp.

Sitting around an old kitchen table brings back many fond memories and also some that aren't so fond. It was there that my dad got a call and we found out his cancer had come back, and it was bad. He just looked at my mother and said the words that I still hear when I think the world has given me more than I can handle, "It ain't no step for a stepper." We all just sat there in silence. For the first time in my life, that table served up something with a bad taste.

Time passed, as did my father, but the table that we sat around after his funeral is still in our family today. If only it could talk and tell of the good times it provided, the bond and the blend of people who had sat at it. Many good recipes were served off that table, and the ones I remember most were made with love and understanding.

Every family needs a good table, and ours had one of the best. It held not only plates but also a family together—better than any glue that was ever used to repair it.

CREAM CHEESE CHICKEN AND GREEN CHILE ENCHILADAS

PREP TIME: I HOUR
TOTAL TIME: I HOUR AND 35 MINUTES
MAKES 8 TO IO ENCHILADAS (4 OR 5 SERVINGS)

---

2 medium bone-in chicken breasts

2 medium bone-in chicken thighs

Salt and black pepper

½ cup chicken broth

I tablespoon butter

I medium yellow onion, diced

½ cup milk

I (8-ounce) block cream cheese, softened

I (4-ounce) can chopped green chilies

CONTINUED

When you cook for a living, it's a real treat when some-one cooks for you. Shannon and I were working on a ranch in northern New Mexico when we had a day off before moving the wagon to another camp. The assistant manager and his wife, Rem and Stormie, invited us back to headquarters for supper. This recipe was inspired by the enchiladas Stormie made for us that night. Every bite was tender and creamy and had a kick of green chilies. Thank ya'll for the hospitality.

1. Preheat the oven to 350°F.

2. Rub both sides of the chicken pieces with salt and pepper. Place the chicken in a 9-x-13-inch casserole dish. Pour the chicken broth into the dish. Cover with tin foil.

3. Bake the chicken for about 1 hour, or until cooked through. Remove the chicken from the oven. Remove the chicken from the broth and set aside to cool. Discard the broth.

4. About 20 minutes before the chicken has finished baking, melt the butter in a 12-inch skillet. Add the onion and cook over medium heat for about 5 minutes, or until tender.

5. Reduce the heat to medium-low and stir in the milk. Heat until warm. Cut the cream cheese into small chunks and add to the skillet. Keep cooking, stirring constantly, until the cheese melts.

6. Stir in the green chilies, cumin, cayenne pepper, ½ teaspoon black pepper, and garlic salt. Taste and adjust the seasonings to taste, if desired. Continue cooking for 2 more minutes to blend the flavors, stirring constantly.

½ teaspoon ground cumin, or
more to taste

½ teaspoon cayenne pepper, or
more to taste

½ teaspoon garlic salt

8 to 10 (8-inch) flour tortillas

Enchilada Sauce
(recipe follows)

1 cup shredded mozzarella
cheese

ENCHILADA SAUCE

PREP TIME: 5 MINUTES
TOTAL TIME: 5 MINUTES
MAKES ABOUT 3½ CUPS

1½ cups sour cream

1½ cups heavy cream

1 (4-ounce) can chopped green
chilies

Pinch of ground cumin

Pinch of cayenne pepper

7. When cool enough to handle, shred the chicken, using a fork. Stir the chicken into the cream cheese mixture.

8. Evenly spoon the chicken mixture onto the flour tortillas, 2 to 3 tablespoons per tortilla, and then tightly roll up.

9. Pour about one third of the enchilada sauce into an 11-x-13-inch casserole dish. Place the enchiladas in the dish and pour the remaining sauce over the top.

10. Bake for 20 to 25 minutes, or until the tortillas soften and the dish is hot. About 5 minutes before the enchiladas are done, sprinkle with the cheese and continue baking until the cheese melts.

11. Sprinkle with additional cayenne pepper and/or cumin (optional) and serve warm.

FOR THE ENCHILADA SAUCE

In a medium bowl, whisk together all the ingredients until smooth.

CHICKEN-AND-SAUSAGE ALMOND CASSEROLE

PREP TIME: 15 MINUTES

TOTAL TIME: 1 HOUR AND 5 MINUTES

MAKES 5 OR 6 SERVINGS

I pound ground sausage

I yellow onion, chopped

½ cup chopped green bell pepper

½ cup chopped celery

1¼ cups Minute White Rice

½ cup slivered almonds

I (10.75-ounce) can cream of chicken soup concentrate

I (14.5-ounce) can chicken broth

I (1-ounce) package Lipton Onion Soup Mix

Salt and black pepper

I'm sure you'll be surprised to hear that this casserole doesn't actually have any chicken in it. But the chicken soup and broth, combined with sausage, onion soup seasonings, and almonds, give it so much flavor that you won't mind at all. It's a great side dish or main course.

1. Preheat the oven to 350°F. Lightly grease a 9-x-13-inch casserole dish.

2. In a 12-inch cast iron skillet, begin browning the sausage over medium heat. As the meat begins to brown, add the onion, green pepper, and celery. Continue cooking until the meat has browned, 8 to 10 minutes.

3. Stir in the rice and almonds. Slowly stir in the chicken soup concentrate, chicken broth, and onion soup mix until well combined. Season with salt and pepper to taste.

4. Scrape the mixture into the casserole dish. Bake for 40 to 50 minutes, stirring occasionally, until the rice is tender. Serve hot.

KEEPER AT THE GATE

AIN'T IT FUNNY HOW WHEN WE GET used to seeing something, we just come to the assumption that it will always be there? It was always at the gate that led down to the bottom pasture. Once tall and strong, it now stood brittle and bent.

I was cooking for a branding during a particular trip down to the bottom pasture, and I noticed it was leaning and looking a bit more weathered than usual. I asked one of the old cowboys on that outfit, "Why hasn't someone ever straightened that old post up or taken it out?" "Well," he said, "after supper when you get the dishes done, I will catch you up on some history."

When the dishes were done, I poured myself a cup of coffee that old Bertha had been warming all day, and sat down with this feller to hear his story. "Now tell me about that one old bois d'arc post that has stood there by that gate," I said. "It's not even in the fence line, it just sits there all alone." He took a draw off the pipe he was smoking and told me, "We call him Sentry, or the Keeper at the Gate. That old post has been there since I was hired on to this place, and that was fifty-three years ago. It has stood there through blowing and drifting snow,

flash floods and heat waves, not to mention the migratory flight of tumbleweeds every fall. I heard that post was put in over a hundred years ago, and we all figured that if it had stood there that long we would just leave it be. It has served as night watchman, messenger, and hitching post. I have left a kerchief tied on it to tell others which pasture I would be in. I knew a feller who once tied a slick yearling to it while he went and got his trailer. You see, that old lone post has earned its place here on the ranch, and we sometimes even tip our hats to that old cuss or tell him adios on our way out."

After everyone had retired to their teepees, I laid there in my bedroll, looking up at the wagon fly that had covered many a cowboy and me for over twenty years. It too was weathered, and so thin in spots you could almost count the stars. I pondered about that old post and the words that feller had told me. That bois d'arc post may not be in any fancy book, but it has great meaning to those who have known it. And no matter what things look like at first glance, not everything that appears a little bent, alone, or used is used up.

BROWN SUGAR-INFUSED PORK LOIN

PREP TIME: 10 MINUTES

TOTAL TIME: 4 HOURS AND 40 MINUTES

MAKES 8 TO 10 SERVINGS

1/3 cup pineapple juice

3 tablespoons light brown sugar

1/2 teaspoon smoked paprika

1 tablespoon tequila

1 tablespoon lime juice

1 teaspoon liquid smoke

1 (4- to 5-pound) pork loin

2 to 3 tablespoons meat tenderizer

1 tablespoon seasoned salt

1 tablespoon lemon pepper

Glaze (*recipe follows*)

I was raised where I had to perform the butchering duties. That's when you quickly learn which meats you like and also which cuts work with different flavors. I have eaten a lot of hog meat, and the two I like the best are bacon and loin. However, many folks make the mistake of overcooking their pork, which causes it to dry out—I mean drier than a wagon wheel rut that ain't seen rain since Noah left. So let's pair a good smoky flavor with brown sugar to create a taste no cowboy will turn down. Glazing this loin along with infusing him will help keep in the moisture for a happier hog.

You'll need a flavor-injector syringe, available in kitchen stores or online.

1. Lightly butter a 9-x-13-inch casserole dish.

2. In a small bowl, whisk together the pineapple juice, brown sugar, and paprika. Set aside.

3. In a separate small bowl, whisk together the tequila, lime juice, and liquid smoke. Rub the mixture evenly over the pork loin. Rub the loin with the meat tenderizer, seasoned salt, and lemon pepper.

4. Draw up the pineapple juice mixture into a flavor-injector syringe. Inject the mixture at several points all over the pork loin.

5. Place the pork in the casserole dish. If the loin has a predominantly fatty side, be sure to place it fat side down. Cover with tin foil and place in the icebox for 2 hours to marinate.

GLAZE

PREP TIME: 5 MINUTES
TOTAL TIME: 5 MINUTES
MAKES ABOUT ½ CUP

⅓ cup plus 2 tablespoons light brown sugar

¼ cup pineapple juice

¼ teaspoon smoked paprika

6. Remove the pork loin from the icebox and let warm to room temperature. About 20 minutes before baking, preheat the oven to 350°F.

7. Keep the pork covered and bake for 1 hour and 30 to 45 minutes, or until the internal temperature is between 140°F and 145°F.

8. Remove the pork from the oven. Increase the oven temperature to 425°F.

9. Brush half of the glaze over the pork loin. Place the pork back in the oven and continue baking for 10 to 15 minutes, or until the glaze has browned.

10. Remove the pork loin and let rest for 8 to 10 minutes. Brush the remaining glaze over the top. Slice the pork and serve warm.

FOR THE GLAZE

Whisk all the ingredients together in a small bowl until smooth.

Every family needs a good table, and ours had one of the best. It held not only plates but also a family together.

BAKED POTATO–STUFFED PORK CHOPS WITH CREAMY WHITE GRAVY

PREP TIME: 20 MINUTES
TOTAL TIME: 1 HOUR AND
15 MINUTES
MAKES 6 SERVINGS

6 (1-inch-thick) bone-in pork chops

Salt and black pepper

Vegetable oil for frying

1 large baking potato, baked

2 tablespoons butter, melted

2 tablespoons sour cream

½ cup chopped green onions

1 teaspoon minced garlic

Creamy White Gravy (*page 43*)

This dish combines two of my favorite things: a big, juicy bone-in pork chop and a loaded baked potato. Make sure to use chops that are thick enough to fit a heaping serving in their pockets. The bone adds flavor and also makes a great handle to get every last bite. Searing the meat first helps seal in all the juiciness.

1. Have your butcher cut a pocket in each of the pork chops for stuffing.

2. Preheat the oven to 375°F. Lightly butter an 11-x-13-inch casserole dish.

3. Rub salt and pepper on both sides of the pork chops.

4. Warm about ½ cup oil in a 12-inch cast iron skillet over high heat.

5. Place 3 pork chops in the skillet. Sear for 2 to 3 minutes per side, or until browned. Repeat with the remaining pork chops, adding more oil, if needed. Set the pork chops aside to cool. Be sure to save the oil in the skillet to use for the Creamy White Gravy. (You may need to add more.)

6. Cut the potato in half. Scoop out the insides and place in a small bowl. Mix in the butter and sour cream, followed by the green onions and garlic. Season with salt and pepper to taste.

7. Evenly spoon the potato mixture into each of the pork-chop pockets. Seal the pork chop openings with butcher string or toothpicks. Place the chops in the casserole dish.

8. Bake for 30 to 35 minutes, or until the pork is golden brown and cooked through. The internal temperature should be about 145°F. Serve warm with the white gravy.

GRILLED PORK CHOPS WITH GREEN CHILE–CHIPOTLE RELISH

PREP TIME: 5 MINUTES

TOTAL TIME: 4 HOURS AND 15 MINUTES

MAKES 4 SERVINGS

1½ tablespoons seasoned salt

1½ tablespoons coarse-ground black pepper

4 (1-inch-thick) bone-in pork chops

Lime juice

Meat tenderizer

Green Chile–Chipotle Relish (*recipe follows*)

I remember the first time I planned a meal on a ranch that included grilled pork chops. It was a cow ranch that raised beef, ate beef, sold beef, and lived beef. I thought to myself, "Will I get a chapping for this?" When I pulled out those thick chops, I got some strange looks, but no one spoke because they all knew the cowboy code: Don't question the cook! After the dishes were in the wreck pan, one of them old-timers came up to me and said, "You're a brave cook to pull out a hog on a cow outfit, but that was the best chop I ever ate." Coating the chops in lime juice and wrapping them in tin foil helps seal in the moisture, because pork can dry out easily.

1. Combine the seasoned salt and pepper in a small bowl. Rub both sides of the pork chops generously with a splash of lime juice. Lightly coat each side of the chops with the meat tenderizer. Repeat with the salt mixture and rub in.

2. Place the chops on a dish, cover, and refrigerate for at least 4 hours, to let the seasonings absorb.

3. Bring the pork chops to room temperature. Preheat a grill to medium-high.

4. Wrap the chops in tin foil and place on the grill over medium-high heat for 4 to 5 minutes per side.

5. Remove the foil from the chops and grill on both sides for 2 to 3 minutes more, or until medium. Be careful not to overcook because pork easily dries out. Spread with the relish and serve immediately.

GREEN CHILE–CHIPOTLE RELISH

PREP TIME: 5 MINUTES
TOTAL TIME: 15 MINUTES
MAKES ABOUT 3½ CUPS

1 (7-ounce) can chipotle peppers in adobo sauce

1 (10-ounce) can **Ro-Tel Diced Tomatoes & Green Chilies**, drained

1 (4-ounce) can green chilies

1 cup sugar

TIP: Be sure to save any unused relish; it goes great on eggs the next morning.

I have to warn you, I like a little kick in my relish. If you like your pig to squeal, leave this recipe just as it is. However, if you like a little less heat, take the seeds out of the chipotle peppers and wash off some of the adobo sauce. Adding a little more sugar will help balance out the heat, and you can also use a mild Ro-Tel.

1. Remove the chipotle peppers from the can and dice.

2. In a medium saucepan, combine the diced chipotle peppers with adobo sauce with the Ro-Tel, green chilies, and sugar. Cook over medium heat for about 10 minutes, stirring frequently, until the sauce thickens slightly and is warmed through. Cool to warm.

SHANNON'S ZESTY MEAT LOAF WITH HONEY HOT SAUCE

PREP TIME: 25 MINUTES
TOTAL TIME: I HOUR AND 15 MINUTES
MAKES 6 TO 8 SERVINGS

---

2 pounds ground beef

3 large eggs

3 tablespoons butter

I purple onion, chopped

I yellow bell pepper, chopped

I orange bell pepper, chopped

2 tablespoons minced garlic

½ cup ketchup

2 tablespoons Worcestershire sauce

I tablespoon prepared horseradish

4 teaspoons hot sauce

CONTINUED

When my wife and I were first married, she claimed she didn't cook and could barely microwave. Being the loving husband that I am, I assured her it was all right, because she married a man who knows his way around the kitchen. One day I came in from shipping cattle and smelled the aroma of spicy meat in the air. You know that scent of peppers mixed with garlic that makes you trot in that direction? Lo and behold, it was Shannon baking a meat loaf. I was pleased to see her cooking but told her right off that my mama made the best one I have ever eaten. Well, folks, I got a new favorite that day, and even my mother said, "This is better than mine."

1. Preheat the oven to 400°F. Butter a baking sheet or turn an 11-x-13-inch casserole dish over, butter the underside, and place upside down on a baking sheet. (This will help drain the grease while the meat loaves are baking.)

2. In a large bowl, mix the meat and eggs together with your hands. Set aside.

3. In a 12-inch cast iron skillet, melt the butter and cook the onion, peppers, and garlic over medium heat, stirring, for about 10 minutes, or until tender.

4. Reduce the heat to low and stir in the ketchup, Worcestershire, horseradish, hot sauce, and cayenne. Season with salt and pepper to taste and simmer for a few minutes to let the flavors combine. You may want to add more of the seasonings to your liking.

5. Remove from the heat and let cool for about 5 minutes.

6. Stir in the milk and slowly begin stirring in the bread crumbs until the mixture is like a thick paste.

½ teaspoon cayenne pepper

Salt and black pepper

⅓ cup milk

I to I ½ cups bread crumbs

Honey Hot Sauce
(*recipe follows*)

HONEY HOT SAUCE

PREP TIME: 2 MINUTES
TOTAL TIME: 2 MINUTES
MAKES ABOUT ½ CUP

½ cup ketchup

2 tablespoons honey

I ½ teaspoons hot sauce

I teaspoon prepared
horseradish

7. With your hands, gently begin mixing the pepper mixture into the meat until combined. You may want to add a few more bread crumbs at this point if the mixture is too wet.

8. Divide the mixture in half and form 2 loaves. Place the loaves on the greased baking sheet or turned-over casserole dish.

9. Spoon the honey sauce over the tops of the loaves and bake for about 50 minutes, or until the meat is cooked through. Serve hot.

FOR THE HONEY HOT SAUCE

In a small bowl, combine all the ingredients until smooth.

MAMA'S ONION MEATBALLS IN CREAMY MUSHROOM GRAVY

PREP TIME: 25 MINUTES
TOTAL TIME: 55 MINUTES
MAKES 5 OR 6 SERVINGS

8 slices thick-cut bacon, cut into ½-inch pieces

2 cups diced assorted sweet mini or orange or yellow bell peppers

1 large yellow onion, diced

2 pounds ground beef

1 tablespoon minced garlic

1 tablespoon smoked paprika

Salt and black pepper

Vegetable oil for cooking, if needed

Mushroom Gravy *(recipe follows)*

I may be prejudiced, but I think my mother made the best meatballs ever invented. The beef was always tender and the gravy a perfect creamy blend. Mama told me the secret to great meatballs was meat that has a good ratio of lean to fat. I use an 80/20 blend. And when out on a ranch, I've used half sausage and half beef. Just don't overbrown them and be sure you have enough gravy to keep them moist on their journey to perfection.

1. Preheat the oven to 350°F. Lightly butter an 11-x-13-inch casserole dish.

2. In a large cast iron skillet, cook the bacon over medium heat until browned, but not crispy. Remove the bacon with a slotted spoon and place on a paper towel. Set aside.

3. Add the peppers and onion to the bacon grease and cook until tender, about 8 minutes. Remove with a slotted spoon, leaving the grease in the pan, and cool slightly.

4. In a medium bowl, crumble the beef. Using your hands, mix in the bacon, onion mixture, garlic, and smoked paprika. Season with salt and pepper to taste.

5. Gently shape the beef mixture into about 24 golf-ball-sized balls. Place the balls in the skillet with the bacon grease and brown the outsides over medium-high heat. Add a little vegetable oil to the skillet, if needed.

6. Pour half the mushroom gravy into the casserole dish. Place the meatballs in the dish and pour the remaining gravy over the meatballs.

7. Bake for 25 to 30 minutes, or until the meatballs are cooked through. Serve hot with the gravy.

PREP TIME: 4 MINUTES

TOTAL TIME: 14 MINUTES

MAKES ABOUT 4 CUPS

2 (10.5-ounce) cans cream of mushroom soup concentrate

1 soup can warm water

¾ cup heavy cream

½ cup sour cream

In a medium saucepan, whisk together all the ingredients until well combined. Cook over medium-low heat, stirring constantly, until warmed through and smooth.

The only difference between good food and great food is the folks we share it with.

CREAMY BEEF AND PARMESAN COMPANY CASSEROLE

Noodles, cream cheese, Parmesan cheese, and beef create an Alfredo casserole that they'll gather around the table for. This is just the type of dish Mama would make when we had company over. It's the kind that is so good that you won't be able to get rid of them!

PREP TIME: 45 MINUTES

TOTAL TIME: 1 HOUR AND 15 MINUTES

MAKES 6 TO 8 SERVINGS

4½ cups spiral noodles

Melted butter or olive oil for the noodles

2 pounds ground beef

2 tablespoons butter

I medium yellow onion, chopped

½ cup chopped green bell pepper

1½ cups sliced mushrooms

2 teaspoons minced garlic

I (8-ounce) block cream cheese, cut into small pieces and softened

1½ cups milk

¼ cup water

½ cup grated Parmesan cheese, plus more for sprinkling

Salt and black pepper

1. Preheat the oven to 350°F. Lightly butter an 11-x-13-inch baking dish.

2. Cook the noodles in a large pot of boiling salted water until tender. Drain and toss with a little melted butter or olive oil to prevent the noodles from sticking together. Set aside.

3. Meanwhile, in a 12-inch cast iron skillet, brown the meat over medium heat. Drain the excess grease and scrape the meat into a large bowl. Set aside.

4. Melt the 2 tablespoons butter in the same skillet. Add the onion, bell pepper, mushrooms, and garlic. Cook over medium-low heat, stirring, for about 10 minutes, or until tender. Add the mixture to the meat and set aside.

5. Add the cream cheese to the same skillet and begin warming over medium-low heat, stirring. As the cream cheese begins to melt, slowly add the milk, water, Parmesan cheese, and salt and pepper to taste. Continue cooking, stirring constantly, for about 5 minutes, or until the mixture is warm and smooth.

6. Mix the noodles and the cream cheese mixture into the meat mixture until well combined. Season with salt and pepper to taste.

7. Scrape the mixture into the baking dish. Sprinkle with additional Parmesan cheese. Bake for 20 to 30 minutes, or until the mixture is bubbling. Serve hot.

THE DANCE OF ST. ELMO'S FIRE

PUSHING CATTLE DOWN THE TRAIL was the job of cowboys, but more than that it was a way of life. It had its rewards, but it also had its many dangers. There are a lot of unmarked graves of young men who met their demise doing what they dreamed of on cattle trails.

Cuts, scrapes, and broken bones were common injuries. But there were two things that worried cowboys more than anything else: river crossings and stampedes. And there were a lot of rivers to cross going up the Chisholm Trail. Some of the most feared were the Red, Canadian, and Cimarron Rivers.

All of these rivers look pretty peaceful, but get a big rain, and that once-gentle flowing stream of water can turn into a raging beast. Two men were usually sent ahead to find a good place to cross, a spot where the banks weren't too steep. Oftentimes the cowboys would give their clothes to the cook before crossing because they would only have one set and they wanted them to stay dry if at all possible.

Drowning was feared by many of those boys during crossings because a spooked horse could buck them off and a lot of those young'uns couldn't swim. A swift current could take them out of sight before anyone even noticed in the frenzy of pushing 2,000 Longhorns.

Possibly even more frightening was that moment when a herd got spooked by weather or even just by a tumbleweed blowing. In an instant, it could happen, and someone would yell out that terrifying cry, "Stampede!"

The cattle stopped for no one. Cowboys would try to get in front of them and bend them into a circle to slow them down. More times than not, someone would be trampled to death by the pounding hooves.

Some stampedes were triggered by a phenomenon known as St. Elmo's fire, which would happen in the driest conditions during a lightning storm. Lightning would strike the ground, and because of static electricity, jump and travel across the cattle's horns like blue fire. The once slow-walking, gentle giants became panicked weapons of mass destruction, running over everything in their way.

So if you ever get to thinking the cowboy life was an easy or romantic occupation, remember the hardships they endured. And the next time you order a steak, lift a glass to the men who made it all possible.

WAGON-WHEEL STEAK

PREP TIME: 15 MINUTES
TOTAL TIME: 1 HOUR AND 20 MINUTES
MAKES 5 SERVINGS

2 ¾ cups all-purpose flour

1 ½ teaspoons black pepper

1 ½ teaspoons seasoned salt

1 ½ teaspoons smoked paprika

½ teaspoon garlic salt

5 (8-ounce) sirloin steaks

Vegetable oil for frying

1 cup milk

1 (10.5-ounce) can cream of mushroom soup concentrate

1 (14.5-ounce) can beef broth

1 large yellow onion, sliced

Salt

Some cuts of meat are so tough I couldn't tenderize them even by running them over with the wagon. But the tougher cuts are always a little cheaper, and that's how this recipe came to be. I sear the steaks first to hold in their flavors. Then I let the oven do the hard work of tenderizing the rascals. Cooking the steaks slowly in a rich sauce of beef broth, cream of mushroom soup, and onion helps tenderize and flavor the meat even more. Now you have a dish that didn't break the bank to make.

1. Preheat the oven to 350°F. Lightly butter a 9-x-13-inch casserole dish or 12-inch cast iron skillet.

2. In a medium bowl, combine 1¾ cups of the flour, the black pepper, seasoned salt, smoked paprika, and garlic salt.

3. Dip each steak in the flour mixture until each side is generously coated.

4. Pour a thin layer of oil into a large skillet. Heat on high heat until very hot. Add the steaks to the skillet and sear for 1½ to 2 minutes on each side, until lightly browned.

5. In a medium bowl, combine the milk, soup concentrate, and beef broth. Sift in the remaining 1 cup flour and mix well.

6. Pour half of the milk mixture into the casserole dish or skillet. Place the steaks in the dish in a single layer. Top with the sliced onion. Pour the remaining milk mixture over the top. Season with salt and pepper to taste.

7. Cover with tin foil and bake for 50 minutes. Remove the foil and continue baking for 10 minutes, or until the meat has cooked through and is tender. Serve hot.

THROWDOWN-WINNING CHICKEN-FRIED STEAK

PREP TIME: 10 MINUTES
TOTAL TIME: 20 MINUTES
MAKES 4 SERVINGS

---

2 ¾ cups all-purpose flour

¼ cup seasoned salt

3 tablespoons lemon pepper

2 tablespoons garlic salt

Canola or peanut oil for frying

4 (5-ounce) pieces tenderized
top or bottom round steak or
cube steak (see Tip)

Golden Fry Batter
(*recipe follows*)

Creamy White Gravy (*page 43*)

It's safe to say I have fixed more chicken-fried steaks than any other person. It's probably the most requested dish from the wagon. First of all, it ain't chicken! It's beef. There are three secrets to this dish: our seasoning, the Golden Fry Batter, and a good cut of meat. I know this is good, because it's been cowboy-approved for years, but it also beat Bobby Flay's recipe in a Throw-down. Chef Flay did give it a great effort, but you can't show up at a cowboy's wagon in the blistering heat, challenge him to a Southern fried specialty, and expect to win.

1. In a medium bowl, combine the flour, seasoned salt, lemon pepper, and garlic salt. Set aside.

2. In a large saucepan, pot, or deep Dutch oven, pour in enough oil to deep-fry the steaks (2½ to 3 inches). Heat the oil over medium-high heat until it reaches about 350°F.

3. Pick up one piece of meat with tongs and dip it into the batter and then into the flour mixture. Be sure both sides are well coated. Repeat, or as I call it, "double baptize." Repeat with the remaining steaks.

4. Fry the pieces for 3 to 4 minutes on each side, or until golden brown. Cool on a wire rack. Serve warm with the gravy.

TIP: "Tenderized" steaks, which are cut from the eye of round, top round, or bottom round, have been mechanically tenderized by the butcher. They look like a cross between a hamburger and a steak. They are also called cube steaks. You can also buy the cuts and tenderize them yourself with a meat tenderizing hammer.

GOLDEN FRY BATTER

PREP TIME: 5 MINUTES
TOTAL TIME: 5 MINUTES
MAKES 3 CUPS

3 tablespoons powdered
whole egg

3 tablespoons powdered milk

1 teaspoon baking powder

½ teaspoon smoked paprika

3 cups warm water

I used to be a milk or buttermilk and egg fan when battering meat to fry, but it seemed that the coating didn't want to stick to the meat as well as I needed it to. This creates a thicker, crispier crust that is the secret to my chicken-fried steak and will work to create a golden crust on meats, veggies, or anything you dream of frying up.

1. In a small bowl, whisk the egg, milk, baking powder, and paprika together.

2. Dissolve the mixture in the water.

TIP: You can replace the Golden Fry Batter with a mixture of 2 cups milk or buttermilk, 2 large eggs, beaten, and 1 teaspoon baking powder.

A man asked me, "When is supper?" "Well, sir," I said, "It's like the monkey said when he got his tail caught in the lawn mower, 'It won't be long now.'"

HOP-ALONG HOMINY CASSEROLE

PREP TIME: 15 MINUTES

TOTAL TIME: 55 MINUTES

MAKES 6 TO 8 SERVINGS

2 (15.5-ounce) cans yellow hominy, drained

1 (4-ounce) can green chilies

4 slices thick-cut bacon, cut into 1-inch pieces

1 medium yellow onion, chopped

1½ cups sour cream

Salt and black pepper

1 cup shredded cheddar cheese

I'd like to believe that it was my good looks and cowboy charisma that won my woman over. Truth be known, it was this dish. Being from up north, my wife had never heard of hominy, and her mother, being Catholic, kept calling it The Homily. But hey, we all need a good blessing every now and then. For you Northerners, hominy is corn that is soaked in an alkali solution and removed from the hull, causing it to swell. You can find hominy in the canned vegetable aisle. It tastes like the flavors of Mexico rolled up into one kernel.

1. Preheat the oven to 350°F. Lightly grease an 8-x-11-inch casserole dish.

2. In a large bowl, combine the hominy and green chilies. Set aside.

3. Place the bacon in a medium cast iron skillet and begin cooking over medium heat. When the bacon begins to brown, add the onion and cook until the bacon is three-quarters done, about 5 minutes. Remove the skillet from the heat and spoon out and discard about half of the bacon grease.

4. Pour the contents of the skillet into the hominy mixture and stir together. Stir in the sour cream. Season with salt and pepper to taste.

5. Scrape the mixture into the casserole dish. Bake for 30 to 40 minutes, or until the mixture is bubbly and the hominy softens slightly.

6. About 5 minutes before the casserole is finished cooking, sprinkle on the cheese and continue cooking until the cheese melts. Serve hot.

GARDEN-HARVEST STIR-FRY

PREP TIME: 10 MINUTES

TOTAL TIME: 40 MINUTES

MAKES 4 TO 6 SERVINGS

4 pieces thick-cut bacon, cut into 1-inch pieces

12 ounces Polish sausage links, sliced

½ cup chopped green bell pepper

½ cup chopped red bell pepper

¾ cup sliced okra

1 yellow squash, sliced

1 yellow onion, diced

2 medium red potatoes, chopped

Olive oil or butter for cooking, if needed

1 tablespoon liquid smoke

Salt and black pepper

When it's harvest time, the garden can overrun you if you don't get to using all that it's producing in a hurry. Get out your basket and get to the garden — or aisle five, whichever it may be. The medley, rich with flavorful and colorful veggies, comes together with a little bacon, sausage, and a hint of smoke like a bunch of cowboys gathered at the wagon at suppertime.

1. In a 12-inch cast iron skillet, cook the bacon and sausage over medium heat until the bacon is three-quarters done. Remove from the skillet and set aside.

2. Add the peppers, okra, squash, onion, and potatoes to the bacon grease, cover, and cook, stirring occasionally, for about 15 minutes, or until tender. You may need to add a little olive oil or butter for more moisture while cooking.

3. Stir in the sausage, bacon, and liquid smoke. Season with salt and pepper to taste. Reduce to a simmer, cover, and continue to cook, stirring occasionally, for 10 minutes to blend the flavors. Serve hot.

Busy? Why I've been busier than a three-legged cat covering up four piles on an ice-covered pond!

BROWN BUTTER AND BACON PASTA

PREP TIME: 30 MINUTES
TOTAL TIME: 30 MINUTES
MAKES 4 TO 6 SERVINGS

8 ounces spaghetti

6 slices thick-cut bacon

1 stick butter

1 teaspoon minced garlic

1½ cups shredded Italian
five-cheese blend

I'm a beef man. But when Shannon came along with this dish, I became a fan. She now fixes it for me on my birthday, so that's saying a lot. The browned butter has a warm nutty flavor, and when you pile on crispy crumbles of bacon, you can't go wrong. Let's just say this recipe is a keeper, and so is she!

1. In a large pot of salted water, boil the spaghetti until tender. Drain and toss the pasta with a little olive oil or butter to prevent the noodles from sticking. Cover and set aside.

2. Meanwhile, brown the bacon in a medium cast iron skillet over medium heat until crispy. Remove from the heat. When the bacon is cool enough to handle, crumble and set aside.

3. Cut the butter into equal pieces and brown in a medium saucepan over medium-low heat, stirring constantly. When it melts, it will begin to froth and bubble. When the bubbling stops, the butter will become light brown and have a nutty aroma. Remove from the heat.

4. Allow the butter to cool for 1 to 2 minutes and then whisk in the garlic. Pour the butter over the pasta and toss until combined. Toss in 1 cup of the cheese.

5. Evenly divide the pasta among four to six dishes. Drizzle each plate with any remaining butter at the bottom of the pan. Top each dish with the crumbled bacon and the remaining cheese. Serve immediately.

TIP: We like to use an Italian cheese blend, but we also use just grated Parmesan when that's all we have on hand.

ROASTED BEAN-STUFFED POBLANO PEPPERS

PREP TIME: 45 MINUTES

TOTAL TIME: I HOUR

MAKES 5 OR 6 PEPPERS;

5 OR 6 SERVINGS

5 or 6 poblano peppers

½ pound ground sausage

I yellow onion, chopped

I (15-ounce) can Ranch Style Beans, drained

½ teaspoon red pepper flakes

½ teaspoon smoked paprika

¼ teaspoon chili powder

¼ teaspoon oregano

½ cup sour cream

I cup shredded mozzarella cheese

Cheese Sauce (*recipe follows*)

CONTINUED

Poblano peppers are one of my favorites, because I like the smoky flavor they have, especially when roasted. Typically, poblanos are a mild pepper. Stuff these rascals full of Ranch Style Beans, sausage, and cheese— they're like a burrito with more flavor than any tortilla can give. I like to season it all with some chili powder and red pepper, but the sour cream tempers it all for full flavor that won't melt your taste buds.

1. Preheat the oven to broil. Line a baking sheet with tin foil.

2. Cut the tops off the peppers and devein. Grease the peppers with butter or spray and place on the baking sheet. Broil for 5 to 10 minutes per side, or until the skins darken and bubble. Remove the peppers from the oven.

3. Reduce the oven to 350°F.

4. When the peppers are cool enough to handle, begin peeling off their skins. You can also run the peppers under cold water to help remove the skins. Be patient with the process because some of those little buggers just don't want to give it up. Set aside.

5. In a large cast iron skillet, crumble the sausage and begin browning over medium heat. When the meat begins to brown, add the onion and continue cooking until the meat completely browns and the onion is soft, stirring occasionally.

6. Reduce the heat to medium-low and stir in the beans, red pepper, paprika, chili powder, and oregano. Cook for 5 minutes, stirring occasionally to blend the flavors. Stir in the sour cream and mozzarella and cook until the cheese melts, stirring occasionally.

CHEESE SAUCE

PREP TIME: 10 MINUTES

TOTAL TIME: 10 MINUTES

MAKES ABOUT 1 ⅓ CUPS

2 tablespoons butter

½ cup heavy cream or milk

6 ounces white American cheese

¼ teaspoon smoked paprika

¼ teaspoon ground cumin

Pinch of red pepper flakes

TIP: Pour the cheese over the peppers right before serving because the cheese will begin to set up quickly as it cools.

7. Spoon the mixture into each pepper until full and return to the baking sheet. Roast for 10 to 15 minutes, or until heated through. Drizzle with the cheese sauce and serve hot.

TIP: The stuffing is usually thick enough that it won't run out of the peppers while roasting. However, you can return the tops to the peppers and secure them with toothpicks while roasting to keep the stuffing inside.

FOR THE CHEESE SAUCE

1. In a small saucepan, melt the butter over medium-low heat. Stir in the cream or milk. Cut the cheese into pieces and add to the saucepan. Continue cooking, stirring frequently, until the cheese melts and is smooth.

2. Stir in the smoked paprika, cumin, and red pepper. Continue cooking for 1 more minute to let the flavors incorporate. Pour over the Roasted Bean–Stuffed Poblano Peppers right before serving.

TIP: If there aren't Ranch Style Beans or Chili Beans at your store, see the tip on page 56.

CHEESY PARTY POTATOES

PREP TIME: 15 MINUTES
**TOTAL TIME: 1 HOUR AND
10 MINUTES**
MAKES 6 TO 8 SERVINGS

1 (2-pound) package frozen
Ore-Ida diced hash brown
potatoes

5 tablespoons butter, melted

1 yellow onion, chopped

1 (10.75-ounce) can cream of
chicken soup concentrate

1 (10.5-ounce) can cream of
celery soup concentrate

2 cups sour cream

2 cups shredded cheddar
cheese

1 teaspoon salt

½ teaspoon black pepper

2 cups crushed cornflakes

This recipe comes from my father-in-law, Skeeter. Let me tell you, folks, this man could be a chef. This is a quick crowd-pleaser that uses frozen hash browns. The star is the cheese, but the celery and chicken soups pull it all together. With a buttery crust, this is a go-to tater recipe.

1. Preheat the oven to 350°F. Lightly butter a 9-x-13-inch casserole dish.

2. Microwave the potatoes for 10 minutes to take the chill off.

3. Heat 1 tablespoon of the butter in a medium skillet. Add the onion and cook over medium-low heat for about 10 minutes, or until tender.

4. In a large bowl, combine the potatoes, onion, soup concentrates, sour cream, cheese, and salt and pepper.

5. Scrape the potato mixture into the casserole dish.

6. In a small bowl, combine the cornflakes and the remaining 4 tablespoons melted butter. Spoon the cornflakes evenly over the casserole.

7. Bake for 45 to 55 minutes, or until the casserole is bubbling. Serve hot.

WHEN IS THERE A DAY OFF?

◆ ◆ ◆ ◆ ◆

OF ALL THE FELLERS I HAVE BEEN around and cooked for, Jake is by far the best. If all hands were like old Jake with his grit and determination, those fellers would have gotten through their chores in half the time. He never missed a day of the fall gathering, and he was always ready at the drop of a hat.

I saw a cow launch him into space one evening and did he go into orbit! But upon re-entry, Jake taught that old horned hussy a lesson in proper cow handling! Now, I'm sure he had days when he ached and hurt, but you never saw it. Every day Jake would crawl out of his bed, stagger to the door of his teepee, and peek out, and I could tell what he was thinking.

My gosh, it looks like it might rain, and I sure don't have a slicker. I've only got one coat and it's dirty. Surely they don't expect me to work outside in these conditions. But I can't let them down; they'd be disappointed. Heck, some might even be mad. I hired on to do a job, and the fellers I'm working with would miss my capabilities. Remember yesterday when some of those cows tried to sneak off on the drive to the pens? They were running like a bunch of grade-school kids at recess! Why, if it weren't for me, those fellers would still be trying to find them in the cedar bushes.

So let's look at the pros and cons of this outfit. They start too early, I have to sleep on the cold ground, and some of them fellers are real grouchy. But it does have its bright spots. The food ain't too bad, I really enjoy being outside (most of the time), and folks say it's in my blood. So let's get started and show them bovines that we mean business! I do hope old Cookie ain't burned the bread. There's nothing I hate worse than a hard, burnt biscuit.

Jessie Ziegler, Jake's owner, had a dear friend in Jake. Jessie told me once that Jake was always on time and never let him down. Not many dogs were allowed under the fly of my wagon, but Jake was an exception. He would lay there under Jessie's chair and never make a sound. He never mooched or tried to steal a bite off someone's plate, and that's more than I can say for some of the cowboys I've fed.

You could tell by the look in Jake's eyes

I do hope old Cookie ain't burned the bread. There's nothing I hate worse than a hard, burnt biscuit.

that he loved two things more than anything in the whole world: working cattle and his owner. You can learn a lot from the way a man treats his dog and the way that dog respects him. There was a great bond between Jake and Jessie. They were family, and I think old Jake might have been the better looking of the two! The more I think about it, Jake was the only one who never complained about what time we ate. Of all the working dogs that I've been around, there were probably none any better mannered or more dependable than old Jake. We could all learn from him. He did his job, never asked for any special treatment, and loved to please those around him. Like my dad said, "Find a job you like to do and do it well." Old Jake sure found his.

SPARKLIN' TATERS

PREP TIME: 25 MINUTES
TOTAL TIME: 1 HOUR AND
5 MINUTES
MAKES 6 TO 8 SERVINGS

5 russet potatoes, sliced into
¼-inch-thick pieces

7 pieces thick-cut bacon, cut
into 1-inch pieces

2 jalapeños, diced

1 large yellow onion, sliced

2 tablespoons minced garlic

Seasoned salt and black pepper

3 to 4 cups lemon-lime soda
(Sprite, 7Up)

"So what makes 'em sparkle?" That's the question I'm always asked. I tell folks it's because they put a sparkle in the eye of anyone who eats them. But you'll see by the ingredients that's not the only reason. I was on the 5R Ranch in the Texas Panhandle, about to prepare the last meal before we had to break camp and go home, when this recipe accidentally came about. I wanted to fry up some taters, but I realized that I didn't have any oil left over. I prowled around to see what I had, and lo and behold, found some Sprite. The soda has a delicious caramelizing effect on the potatoes.

TIPS: Covering the dish will keep the liquid from boiling out, but feel free to add more soda while cooking if the potatoes don't have enough moisture to soften. You can also use Mountain Dew soda.

1. Preheat the oven to 400°F. Lightly butter an 11-x-13-inch casserole dish or a 12-inch Dutch oven.

2. Place the potatoes in cold water and set aside.

3. Place the bacon in a large cast iron skillet and cook over medium heat for about 4 minutes, or until it begins to brown. Add the jalapeños, onion, and garlic. Reduce the heat to medium-low and continue cooking, stirring, until the bacon is three-quarters done (not crisp) and the vegetables soften, about 8 minutes. Remove from the heat.

4. Drain the potatoes. Place a layer of potatoes in the casserole dish. Cover with half of the bacon mixture and sprinkle with the seasoned salt and pepper to taste. Repeat with the remaining ingredients. Pour the soda over the entire dish until about half full.

5. Cover the dish with tin foil and bake for 20 minutes. Remove the foil and stir. Replace the foil and continue baking for about 20 more minutes, or until the potatoes are tender. Reseason with salt and pepper, if desired. Serve hot.

CHEESY GREEN BEANS WITH ROASTED RED PEPPERS

PREP TIME: 10 MINUTES
TOTAL TIME: 55 MINUTES
MAKES 6 TO 8 SERVINGS

1 (16-ounce) package or 4 cups frozen green beans

1 (12-ounce) jar roasted red peppers and caramelized onions

2 teaspoons minced garlic

1 (10.5-ounce) can cream of mushroom soup concentrate

1 teaspoon salt

½ teaspoon black pepper

4 ounces Velveeta cheese

Almost everyone has had green bean casserole—that old standby with mushroom soup and French onions on top, usually served during major holidays. Shannon and I have revived my mother's recipe, adding cheese along with some red peppers for color and flavor.

1. Preheat the oven to 350°F. Lightly butter an 8-x-11-inch casserole dish.

2. Microwave the green beans for 5 minutes to take the chill off.

3. In a large bowl, stir together the green beans, peppers and onions, garlic, soup concentrate, salt, and black pepper.

4. Scrape the mixture into the baking dish. Cut the Velveeta into small cubes and place evenly on top of the casserole.

5. Bake for about 45 minutes, or until the beans are tender. Twenty minutes into baking, or when the cheese begins to melt, remove from the oven and stir. Stir the casserole a few more times during the baking to incorporate the cheese. Serve hot.

TIP: I prefer fresh or frozen beans because they're more flavorful and hold up better than canned. If you use fresh green beans, boil them first for 5 to 10 minutes, just until tender. For canned green beans, decrease the baking time to about 25 minutes, or until the cheese is fully melted and the casserole has warmed through.

CHEESY ONION RING BAKE

PREP TIME: 15 MINUTES
TOTAL TIME: 40 MINUTES
MAKES ABOUT 6 SERVINGS

---

1 stick butter

2 tablespoons olive oil

2 medium yellow onions, sliced and separated into rings

Salt and black pepper

1 cup shredded mozzarella or Swiss cheese

1 (10.75-ounce) can cream of chicken soup concentrate

1 tablespoon red wine vinegar

½ heaping cup bread crumbs

I have to admit, the first time Shannon tried this on me I was a little gun-shy—sort of like a broncy colt on a cold morning. I had to warm up to it. I'd never cooked with red wine vinegar, because I typically use apple cider or balsamic. But that vinegar gives the dish a more subtle tart taste, which lends a hand to its creamy friends, mozzarella and cream of chicken soup. The recipe is a take on one from my father-in-law, Skeeter.

1. Preheat the oven to 350°F. Lightly butter an 8-x-11-inch casserole dish.

2. Melt the ½ stick of the butter in a 12-inch skillet. Add the olive oil and onions and cook, stirring occasionally, over medium-low heat for about 10 minutes, or just until the onions are tender. Remove from the heat.

3. Spoon the onions into the baking dish, leaving the excess butter and olive oil in the skillet. Lightly salt and pepper the onions and sprinkle with the cheese.

4. Pour the soup concentrate into the skillet. Add the vinegar and stir to combine. Season with salt and pepper to taste.

5. Pour the soup mixture evenly over the onions.

6. Melt the remaining ½ stick butter in a small saucepan. In a small bowl, combine the bread crumbs and the butter. Sprinkle the bread crumbs over the onion mixture.

7. Bake for 20 to 25 minutes, or until the mixture becomes bubbly and the topping browns slightly. Serve warm.

MASHED BROWN SUGAR SWEET POTATOES

- - - ◆ ◆ ◆ - - -

PREP TIME: 45 MINUTES

TOTAL TIME: 1 HOUR AND 20 MINUTES

MAKES 5 TO 6 SERVINGS

◆ ◆ ◆

3 or 4 sweet potatoes, peeled and quartered

2 cups light brown sugar

2 sticks butter, melted

½ cup half-and-half

2 large eggs, lightly beaten

⅓ cup all-purpose flour

⅓ cup cornbread mix

1½ cups chopped pecans

¼ cup warm water

Most folks have a sweet tater recipe that they use over the holidays, but I get tired of the marshmallow tradition. As they say in my country, though, this dog will hunt, meaning this is a great twist on a classic dish. Let's add brown sugar instead of marshmallow for a rich sweetness. The cornmeal topping, coupled with the pecans, makes a home-run crust.

1. Preheat the oven to 350°F. Lightly butter an 8-x-11-inch casserole dish.

2. Place the potatoes in a large saucepan or pot and cover with water. Bring the water to a boil over high heat. Boil the potatoes about 25 minutes, or until they are fork-tender.

3. Remove the potatoes from the heat and drain. Mash until smooth.

4. Beat in 1 cup of the brown sugar, 1 stick of the butter, the half-and-half, and the eggs. Mix well.

5. Scrape the potato mixture into the casserole dish and spread evenly.

6. In a medium bowl, stir together the remaining 1 cup brown sugar, the flour, cornbread mix, and pecans. Stir in the remaining 1 stick butter and the warm water. Mix well.

7. Spread the brown sugar mixture evenly over the potatoes.

8. Bake for 30 to 35 minutes, or until the top is golden brown and a light crust forms. Serve hot.

SMOOTH-AS-BUTTER CREAMY CORN

PREP TIME: 15 MINUTES
TOTAL TIME: 15 MINUTES
MAKES 4 TO 5 SERVINGS

1 (16-ounce) bag frozen corn kernels

½ cup heavy cream

½ cup milk

3 tablespoons sugar

1 teaspoon salt, plus more to taste

½ teaspoon black pepper, plus more to taste

2 tablespoons butter, melted

2 tablespoons all-purpose flour

This was always a Thanksgiving tradition in my mother's kitchen, but we break it out now to impress company. Folks will think you went to a lot of trouble putting it together, because it's too good to be this simple. Frozen corn, cream, and butter with a little love transform plain ole corn into a quick and easy side dish.

1. In a large saucepan, combine the corn, cream, milk, sugar, salt, and pepper. Cook over medium-high heat until the mixture comes to a boil, stirring occasionally.

2. Reduce the heat and simmer for 5 minutes. Stir in the butter and flour until the mixture thickens.

3. Remove from the heat. Season with salt and pepper. Serve hot.

YEAST ROLLS

PREP TIME: I HOUR AND
35 MINUTES
TOTAL TIME: I HOUR AND
50 MINUTES
MAKES 20 TO 24 ROLLS

¾ cup milk

½ cup sugar

½ stick butter, cut into
tablespoons

I teaspoon salt

½ cup warm water

2 (¼-ounce) packages
rapid-rise yeast

I large egg

3½ to 4 cups all-purpose flour,
plus a little more if needed

TIP: These rolls can also
be placed in muffin pans to
bake.

I've always liked a good yeast roll, and this recipe creates a rich one with a buttery flavor. We made these a lot for company when I was young. Get 'em while they're hot, 'cause the pan will be empty before they have time to cool off.

1. Butter a 9-x-13-inch baking pan or a 12-inch cast iron skillet.

2. In a small saucepan, warm the milk, sugar, butter, and salt over medium-low heat until warmed through and the butter has melted. Remove from the heat and cool to lukewarm.

3. In a large bowl, whisk together the warm water and yeast until the yeast dissolves. Whisk in the egg, then the milk mixture.

4. With a mixer, beat in 2 cups of the flour until smooth.

5. Stir in the remaining 1½ to 2 cups flour until it forms a soft dough. Be sure the dough isn't too sticky.

6. Cover the dough and let sit in a warm place for 45 minutes, or until it has risen slightly. Knead down the dough slightly and knead in more flour if it is too sticky.

7. Flour your hands and pinch off the dough into golf-ball-sized pieces. Place the balls close together on the baking pan or skillet.

8. Cover the rolls with a buttered piece of wax paper and place over a pot of boiling water. Let rise for about 30 minutes, or until nearly doubled in size. Meanwhile, preheat the oven to 400°F.

9. Bake for 15 minutes, or until a light golden brown.

CRITTERS IN CAMP

Amigo and Boo

These pups belong to my friend, Kye. Amigo is a Blue Lacy and a good copilot. He sits right between Kye and me when we are driving the wagon, keeping an eye out for anything that might sneak up on us.

Amigo's buddy, Boo, is a border collie who needs a couple of new hearing aids. Kye says he just has selective hearing. He doesn't like driving much, but he sure is fond of napping when we move the wagon between camps.

Bonehead the Beagle

Shannon adopted this rescue dog, but I'm not sure who rescued whom. Built for tracking rabbits, Bonehead can also track a biscuit pretty well. He has many titles: taste tester, pot licker, food critic, and most of all, camp security—if it's not past his bedtime.

Mouse in the House

A lady hired me to bring the wagon to a shopping mall as a backdrop for a Western fashion show. I told her not to mess around in any of the drawers. As I opened one up to show her, a mouse jumped out and scurried across that mall at warp speed. She screamed at the top of her lungs, "I'm paying you how much for this?" I replied, "Not enough, Ma'am, but I threw the mouse in for free."

Rattlesnake

It's amazing how an old rattler can blend into a woodpile. I guess I've been fortunate because there have been quite a few in camp over the years, and I haven't been bit yet. The most snakes I've killed at one camp were four at the Goodnight pens on the JA Ranch.

Skunk

Breakfast brings the aroma of frying bacon in the air. But on this early morning on a ranch near Abilene, Texas, a different smell was in the air. While frying the bacon, I glanced over and saw a mama skunk and

Wilbur the Hummingbird
FACING, TOP TO BOTTOM:
Amigo and Boo, Bonehead the Beagle, Rattlesnake

her five babies. I knew if I spooked her, she could ruin breakfast. It was probably only forty-five seconds, but it felt like five minutes of our staring at each other. She finally turned and they went on their way, taking their scent with them.

Ticks

I was on a ranch in eastern Oklahoma where the ticks grow bigger than snapping turtles. That spring those fellers made a home on my little white legs. I would sit in my teepee with a flashlight and a pair of tweezers and pull off about thirty every night. It looked like I had chickenpox after I got through. If you find yourself in that situation, put sulfur powder around the bottoms of your britches' legs and waistline to repel the ticks and chiggers.

Wilbur the Hummingbird

Shannon and I couldn't believe our eyes when Wilbur showed up in camp. We were in the middle of nowhere in New Mexico. It was a very dry year: not a flower blooming in sight. We fixed him a glass of sweet tea, and I think he thought he had hit the mother lode. I've never seen a hummingbird land, and he was a right friendly feller as he frequently hovered by our shoulders while we were working. He came back every day for four days until we had to move camp.

LET OUT THE CINCHES
(DESSERT)

WHEN THE DAY'S CHORES ARE done and it's time to unsaddle the horses, the first thing we do is let out the cinches. A cinch is a band that fits under a horse's belly to hold and keep the saddle in place. Most times during riding and working, the cinch will be pulled pretty tight, but sometimes a cowboy will loosen it to let the horse catch his breath and relax for a bit.

It's the same way with folks after a big meal, when their eyes seem to be a little bigger than their stomach, and they are wishing they had worn those sweatpants with the elastic band. But hold on, 'cause here comes someone toting out dessert, and their sweet tooth overrides all rational thought. Well, we better loosen the belt a few notches, 'cause we're going to need a little more room in these jeans.

I'll confess this is my favorite part of any meal. I sure don't mind letting the belt out and eating something sweet.

It's the same way after supper at the wagon. When those boys think they're full and tell me they can't hold any more or they'll bust, I'll crack a lid on a Dutch oven full of cobbler or cake and somehow they seem to make room. They might whine a little when it's all over, but they will admit it was worth it. My mother always told me that complementing supper with a dessert that people will make themselves miserable over turns a good meal into a great one.

THE RECIPES

BREAD PUDDING WITH WHISKEY CREAM SAUCE

PREP TIME: 10 MINUTES
TOTAL TIME: 55 MINUTES
MAKES ABOUT 12 SERVINGS

2 cups milk

1½ cups sugar

3 large eggs

1 stick butter, melted

1 teaspoon vanilla extract

1 teaspoon cinnamon, or more to taste

1 teaspoon nutmeg, or more to taste

10 regular-sized hamburger buns

Whiskey Cream Sauce (*recipe follows*)

If you have to choose just one thing to make in this cookbook, this is it. I can't believe I'm even giving y'all this recipe! I have kept it a secret in my back pocket for many years, not even sharing it with my own family. I was cooking for a rodeo in Biloxi, Mississippi, when we went to a restaurant that had the best bread pudding I'd ever eaten. I called the chef out to try to get the recipe. Turned out he was a sourdough biscuit fan, so I tried to swap recipes with him, but he must have been a horse trader from way back, because he didn't give in. It took me years to re-create it, and I think I like it even better than his. My version has a cinnamon French-toast flavor with a dense consistency. Typically bread pudding is made with old bread, but I use hamburger buns, which give it a fresher, lighter taste.

1. Preheat the oven to 350°F. Lightly butter an 8-x-11-inch baking pan with a rack in the middle.

2. In a large bowl, whisk together the milk, sugar, and eggs until smooth. Slowly whisk in the butter, vanilla, cinnamon, and nutmeg. If you like the flavor of nutmeg, you can add a few more shakes.

3. Tear a bun into approximately 1-inch pieces and add to the wet mixture. Repeat, using half of the buns.

4. Mash the buns with a spoon into the wet mixture until moistened. Tear the remaining buns and add to the mixture. Mash until combined, but don't mash them so much that the mixture turns to mush. The bread should be completely moistened with some bun pieces still retaining most of their shape. Add more cinnamon or nutmeg, if desired. Scrape the mixture into the baking pan.

WHISKEY CREAM SAUCE

PREP TIME: 5 MINUTES

TOTAL TIME: 6 MINUTES

MAKES ABOUT 3 CUPS

I cup sugar

I stick butter, melted

2 cups heavy cream

¼ to ½ cup whiskey

TIP: If you like the whiskey taste, do not bring the sauce to a boil. Instead, simply allow the mixture to warm through and serve.

5. Bake for about 45 minutes, or until the pudding is sponge-like and springs back when touched in the middle. Feel free to make a judgment call on the baking time. You don't want it to bake completely through like a cake; remember it's bread *pudding.* You can err on the side of not cooking the pudding quite as long, because it will set up a little more after it cools.

6. Drizzle or drench with Whiskey Cream Sauce. Serve warm or at room temperature.

FOR THE WHISKEY CREAM SAUCE

The bread pudding is really just an excuse to taste this. In fact some of you may want to scratch the pudding and head straight for the sauce! My friend Chris Morton calls it "Goes Over Sauce" 'cause it will go over nearly anything and make it good. It is also great in your coffee the next morning.

Combine all the ingredients in a medium saucepan. Bring to a boil and boil for 1 minute. Serve warm.

STEWED APPLES

PREP TIME: 10 MINUTES

TOTAL TIME: 40 MINUTES

MAKES 6 SERVINGS

6 apples, peeled, cored, and sliced

1 stick butter, melted

1 cup sugar

¼ cup light brown sugar

2 teaspoons cinnamon

½ cup water

When you walk into a kitchen, the aroma of stewing apples and cinnamon feels like home and love. Growing up, we had an apple tree outside, and Mama would use apples in everything. I began cooking this on ranches, and it quickly became a cowboy favorite. I think that's because it's a comfort dish that reminded those fellers of home even if we were fifty miles off the beaten path. Also try in the Caramel Apple Cinnamon Cups (page 223).

1. Stir all the ingredients together in a large saucepan or pot until combined. Bring to a light boil over medium heat and boil for 5 minutes, stirring occasionally.

2. Reduce the heat to medium, cover, and continue cooking, stirring occasionally, for an additional 15 to 20 minutes, or until the apples are tender.

3. Remove from the heat. Let cool slightly. Serve warm.

TIP: You can use your favorite apple for these, but I prefer ones on the sweeter side like Fuji or Gala.

HOT DAMN! FRIED BANANAS

PREP TIME: 5 MINUTES
TOTAL TIME: 10 MINUTES
MAKES 6 SERVINGS

I cup sugar

I tablespoon cinnamon

3 bananas, peeled

I stick butter

I cup DeKuyper Hot Damn! Cinnamon Schnapps Liqueur

Vanilla ice cream for serving

This is a treat I cook on ranches in the fall of the year. The name has got the two things you like most: liquor and "fried." The Hot Damn! schnapps adds a bold cinnamon bite. If you're like me, and appreciate the bite, save your match and don't burn the liquor out.

1. In a small bowl, combine the sugar and cinnamon. Set aside.

2. Cut the bananas in half and then cut again, lengthwise.

3. Toss the bananas in the sugar mixture until generously coated. Leave them in the mixture.

4. In a large cast iron skillet, melt the butter over medium-low heat. Add the bananas and fry on each side for 1 to 2 minutes, or until softened slightly.

5. Pour the schnapps into the skillet and lightly stir the bananas around to absorb some of the flavor. Light the schnapps on fire. It should flame off quickly.

6. Remove from the heat. Place the bananas over ice cream and drizzle with the remaining sauce from the skillet. Serve immediately.

There are a lot of cow trails in life. Be sure to look where you're going or you might step into something you didn't want.

CHERRY CRESCENT-ROLL BARS

PREP TIME: 10 MINUTES

TOTAL TIME: 30 MINUTES

MAKES ABOUT 15 BARS

1 (21-ounce) can cherry pie filling

1 teaspoon almond extract

2 (8-ounce) cans crescent rolls

½ stick butter, melted

½ cup sugar

1 (8-ounce) block cream cheese, softened

Have you ever been in a bind and needed to pull together a quick dessert for surprise guests? This one, with its layers of flaky crescent rolls, cream cheese, and cherry pie filling, will save the day. You can also substitute canned biscuits for the crescent dough or your favorite pie filling for the cherry filling.

1. Preheat the oven to 350°F with a rack in the middle. Butter a 9-x-13-inch baking pan.

2. In a small bowl, combine the pie filling and almond extract. Set aside.

3. Unroll 1 can of crescent rolls along the bottom of the pan, pressing it to the edges. Brush the dough with half of the melted butter and then sprinkle with half of the sugar.

4. Place the cream cheese in a microwave-safe bowl and microwave for about 1 minute, or just until it begins to melt. With an electric mixer, beat the cheese until smooth. Spread evenly over the dough and top with the cherry mixture.

5. Unroll the second can of crescent rolls and place over the top of the dish, stretching it to the edges. Brush with the remaining butter and sprinkle with the remaining sugar.

6. Bake for 20 minutes, or until golden brown. Let cool slightly before cutting into bars. Serve warm or at room temperature.

BLUEBERRY-ALMOND BUTTER BARS

PREP TIME: 10 MINUTES

TOTAL TIME: 1 HOUR AND
10 MINUTES

MAKES ABOUT 15 BARS

1½ (21-ounce) cans blueberry
pie filling

1½ teaspoons almond extract

2 sticks butter, softened

1¾ cups sugar

3 large eggs

1 teaspoon vanilla extract

2½ cups all-purpose flour

Glaze (*recipe follows*)

**TIP: It works best to bake
this in a clear glass dish so
you can easily determine
when the bottom has baked
to a rich golden brown.**

*This was one of the first desserts my wife made for me,
and it's been a favorite ever since. It's a wonder that
the batter ever makes it to the oven, because I try to
eat it when Shannon isn't looking. We have also made
this with cherry pie filling for an equally good pairing.*

1. Preheat the oven to 350°F with a rack in the middle.
Butter a 9-x-13-inch baking pan, preferably Pyrex.

2. In a small bowl, combine the blueberry pie filling and
½ teaspoon of the almond extract. Set aside.

3. In a large bowl, cream together the butter and sugar
for 1 to 2 minutes, or until light and fluffy. Slowly beat in
the eggs. Add the vanilla extract and the remaining 1 teaspoon almond extract.

4. Slowly beat in the flour until combined.

5. Scrape the batter into the pan, reserving ⅓ to ½ cup of
the batter. Evenly spread the blueberry mixture over the
batter. Dollop the reserved batter evenly over the filling.

6. Bake for 50 to 60 minutes. (You may want to rotate between the bottom and middle racks to even out the cooking.) The bars are done when a toothpick inserted near
the edge comes out clean and the bottom is browned. The
sides of the dish will begin to brown before the center is
finished. You may want to err on the side of not cooking
the center until completely done because the bars will set
up slightly as they cool. Allow the dish to cool to room temperature. Drizzle with the glaze, cut, and serve.

GLAZE

PREP TIME: 5 MINUTES
TOTAL TIME: 5 MINUTES
MAKES ABOUT ½ CUP

2 tablespoons milk or heavy cream

1¼ cups powdered sugar

1 teaspoon almond extract

Slowly whisk the milk into the powdered sugar until you achieve the desired consistency. Whisk in the almond extract.

Life is simple; people complicate it.

A COWBOY'S CODE

The chuck wagon cook is second in command behind the ranch manager, but around the wagon, the cook is boss. Cowboys obey the cook and his rules, and should never come under the fly of the wagon without being invited by the cook.

The spot between the chuck box lid and the fire is known as the cook's domain and sacred ground. Any good cowboy knows only the cook is allowed there.

A cowboy should never ride his horse close to camp, which would be called "dusting the camp."

A good cowboy always rinses his plate and puts it in the wreck pan after eating.

A cowboy should never ride in front of another man on a drive and always waits until everyone else goes through a gate and the gate is closed before riding out.

A white rag tied in the corner of the fly notifies cowboys from a distance that there is a lady present in camp and there should be no bad language.

A good cowboy always tips his hat to a lady.

It is bad luck to remove your hat and place it on a bed.

A cowboy should always unsaddle, water, and feed his horse at the end of the day before taking care of himself.

BROWN SUGAR– COCONUT BARS

PREP TIME: 10 MINUTES
TOTAL TIME: 40 MINUTES
MAKES ABOUT 15 BARS

1 pound light brown sugar

4 large eggs

2½ cups shredded coconut

1 (7.5-ounce) package buttermilk biscuit mix

2 teaspoons vanilla extract

1 cup chopped pecans
(*optional*)

TIP: I've also used 1½ cups instant buttermilk pancake mix in place of the biscuit mix.

Not a cake, not a cookie, but a moist and chewy brown sugar brownie. I love the sweet maple-like flavor brown sugar has, and if you're a fan of coconut, come over to my house and we'll eat these all day long. They just might take the place of your favorite chocolate brownie.

1. Preheat the oven to 350°F with a rack in the middle. Butter a 9-x-13-inch baking pan.

2. In a large bowl, beat the brown sugar and eggs together until smooth.

3. Slowly beat in the coconut, biscuit mix, and vanilla until combined. Stir in the pecans, if using.

4. Pour the batter into the pan. Bake for 25 to 30 minutes, or until golden brown and the bars set up. Feel free to make a judgment call on the baking time because the bars will set up slightly more as they cool.

A good friend will give you the shirt off of his back, but a true friend will put a twenty-dollar bill in the pocket.

RASPBERRY-APPLE CRUMBLE

PREP TIME: 10 MINUTES
TOTAL TIME: 50 MINUTES
MAKES 6 TO 8 SERVINGS

1 cup all-purpose flour

¾ cup sugar

¼ cup light brown sugar

1 stick butter, softened

4 sweet apples, peeled, cored, and sliced

1 (3-ounce) package raspberry Jell-O

Vanilla ice cream for serving (*optional*)

This is a pairing made in heaven. I prefer to use a sweet apple (Gala or Fuji), which couples perfectly with the tartness of the raspberry Jell-O. Sprinkle with a butter and brown sugar crumble mixture and you'll have a dessert that can stand alone. Or make it really special and serve with ice cream.

1. Preheat the oven to 350°F with a rack in the middle. Butter a 9-x-13-inch baking pan.

2. In a medium bowl, combine the flour, sugar, and brown sugar. Cut in the butter with a fork until crumbly.

3. Place the apples in the pan. Sprinkle the Jell-O packet evenly over the apples, then sprinkle with the crumble mixture.

4. Bake for about 40 minutes, or until bubbling slightly around the edges and the crumble begins to brown. Serve warm alone or as a warm topping over vanilla ice cream.

Your word is like a gate in a fence. If the gate is weak, the fence ain't worth much.

COWBOY BANANA SPLIT COBBLER

PREP TIME: 15 MINUTES
TOTAL TIME: 60 MINUTES
MAKES 8 TO 10 SERVINGS

---

1 heaping cup sliced
strawberries, thawed if frozen

1 banana, sliced

1 (15-ounce) can sliced peaches
in heavy syrup

2 cups all-purpose flour

2 cups sugar

4 teaspoons baking powder

1 teaspoon salt

½ teaspoon cinnamon

2 cups milk

1 teaspoon vanilla extract

1 stick butter, melted

1 to 2 cups Hershey's Kisses

**TIP: Frozen strawberries
create more juice for
better flavor.**

It was early June, but the days were already getting hot and long. One of the cowboys came up to me and said, "Kent, it sure would be nice to have an ice cream banana split right now!" There ain't no way to keep ice cream on a wagon in June, but I got to digging around and found some canned peaches, strawberries, and Hershey kisses that I had kept hidden. One of the ranch wives brought down some bananas, and I was able to put together a cowboy's take on a banana split.

1. Preheat the oven to 350°F with a rack in the middle. Lightly butter an 11-x-13-inch baking pan.

2. In a large bowl, combine the strawberries, banana, and peaches and their juice. Set aside.

3. In a large bowl, whisk together the dry ingredients. Whisk in the milk and vanilla.

4. Pour the melted butter into the baking pan. Pour the batter into the pan.

5. Spoon the fruit mixture with the juice evenly on top of the batter.

6. Bake for 40 to 45 minutes, or until about three quarters of the cobbler has baked through like a cake and is golden brown on top. The rest should be slightly gooey because it will set as it cools. I like to poke the cobbler in several spots with a spoon about halfway through, to help even out the baking.

7. About 10 minutes before the cobbler is done, place the Hershey's Kisses on the top, pushing them in slightly. Continue baking until the cobbler is done. Serve warm or at room temperature.

THE RED VELVET MASSACRE

IT WAS A TYPICAL SPRING WORKS on a ranch in central Texas, and I was going to be cooking three meals a day for fifteen cowboys. I was ready for a week of fine dining and luxurious accommodations.

I got to camp the day before work began to get settled in. The first thing was to scope out the woodpile: Was there enough? Had any critters made a home in it? The second item of business was to get the homestead claimed and set up my teepee. Any good real estate agent knows it's about location, location, location. In my business, prime location means no ant beds, cactus, or cow piles.

After a quick survey, I found a pretty little spot with a short commute to work, only about forty yards to the wagon. After settling in, I was off to bed at 8:30 P.M. The first night is always short, and after looking at the clock every forty-five minutes, at 3:45 A.M., I decided it was time to get up and build a fire. With a deep breath, I took in a good sunrise, and it was off to cooking. I got the sourdough biscuits all huddled together in the Dutch oven and put them on the coals to bake. I fried the bacon up, and breakfast commenced at 5 A.M.

The crew was a polite bunch, but they were grabbing food faster than a Kmart shopper at a blue-light special. There wasn't even a lick of gravy left—they put it on everything! I even saw one feller use it as coffee creamer.

I had never fed them before, but they were a healthy-looking bunch and they could eat. Two of those boys—one who looked like Paul Bunyan and the other like Babe the Blue Ox—hollered as they left, "No one has ever been able to fill us up at the same time." Well, I like a bunch that can eat, so they were in for a treat at noon. Thick and crispy chicken-fried steak, garlic mashed taters, gravy, "whistle" berries—pinto beans—with a bite, and buttermilk biscuits. I'll get these fellers full!

It was no surprise when they came in and acted like they had never seen food before. Once again, they licked those plates clean enough to put right back on the shelf. I had a bunch of growing boys on my hands. Don't let the tall, skinny ones fool you—they've got hollow legs that can hold a lot of biscuits. I was going to have to pull out the big guns for that night's supper. My weapon of choice was 1¼-inch-thick, juicy, mesquite-grilled rib eyes, and I wasn't stopping there! Loaded baked potatoes, hominy and green chile casserole, sourdough biscuits, and to seal the deal, a double-decker red velvet cake for dessert.

It was suppertime, and I looked up to see the crew walking toward me in slow motion, like in an old gunfighter Western movie. I guess my draw was a little quicker than theirs, because by the end of supper, I had fifteen cowboys swelled up like blue ticks sucking on a hound dog. There was even half a cake left. Clenching their bellies like they had been gut-shot, they all agreed they'd eat the cake for breakfast.

With the dishes washed and the kitchen clean, I covered the cake with a bean pot and put a rock on it to keep out the night critters. I headed to my hacienda and was asleep before my head hit the pillow. At about 1 A.M., a loud noise startled me out of my coma. I have heard a lot of things at night in a cow camp, but this was different: dishes banging and lots of hissing. I slipped on my boots and grabbed a flashlight. As I crept closer to the wagon, whatever was going on intensified. There was growling, screaming, and fur flying. I pointed

my light into the darkness and saw two raccoons. One had the other in a chokehold. I thought I had stumbled upon a massacre: There was blood everywhere. But after rubbing my eyes, I realized someone had murdered the red velvet cake!

I thought I had spotted all the culprits when I heard something rustling behind me. I swung my light over and found another hoodlum. An opossum froze there on top of the chuck box. He was covered with cake and icing and was missing a little fur. With a little gentle persuasion and a shovel, I got all my uninvited guests cleared out of camp. I cleaned up what I could and tried to get some sleep with what was left of the night.

You never know who or what is going to come into camp looking for a bite. But be it man or critter, I've never sent anyone away on an empty stomach.

WANDI'S RED VELVET CAKE

PREP TIME: 10 MINUTES
TOTAL TIME: 40 MINUTES
MAKES 1 LAYER CAKE
(12 TO 16 SERVINGS)

2 tablespoons red food coloring

1 tablespoon sweetened cocoa

½ cup Crisco

1½ cups sugar

2 large eggs

1 cup buttermilk

2¼ cups all-purpose flour

¼ teaspoon salt

1½ teaspoons vanilla extract

1 tablespoon white vinegar

1 teaspoon baking soda

Icing (*recipe follows*)

This was the first red cake I'd ever seen in my life, and I sure thought it was something fancy. Wandi Beth is a dear family friend and her food never disappoints. This cake and the icing have a rich, homemade flavor.

1. Preheat the oven to 350°F with racks in the middle and upper third. Butter and flour two 8- or 9-inch cake pans.

2. In a small bowl, whisk the food coloring and cocoa together to form a paste.

3. In a large bowl, cream together the Crisco, sugar, and eggs. Add the red paste and mix well.

4. Mix in the buttermilk. Slowly mix in the flour and salt.

5. In a small bowl, combine the vinegar, vanilla, and baking soda until blended. Stir into the cake mixture.

6. Pour the batter evenly into the two cake pans. Bake for about 30 minutes, or until a toothpick inserted into the center comes out clean. Allow the cakes to cool completely before icing. Serve at room temperature.

Even a blind hog finds an acorn every once in a while.

ICING

PREP TIME: 15 MINUTES
TOTAL TIME: 25 MINUTES
MAKES ABOUT 2 CUPS

5 tablespoons all-purpose flour

1 cup milk

½ stick butter, softened

½ cup Crisco

1 cup sugar

1. In a medium saucepan, cook the flour and milk over medium heat until thick, stirring constantly. Remove from the heat and let cool to room temperature.

2. Beat the mixture with an electric mixer for 2 minutes. Add the butter, Crisco, and sugar and beat for an additional 4 minutes.

"ICE CREAM" POUND CAKE WITH MIXED BERRIES

PREP TIME: 10 MINUTES
TOTAL TIME: 20 MINUTES
MAKES ABOUT 5 SERVINGS

---

1 (12-ounce) package frozen mixed berries, thawed

2 to 4 tablespoons plus ⅓ cup sugar

1 cup heavy cream

1 large egg

1 teaspoon vanilla extract

2 tablespoons butter

Lemon-Almond Pound Cake (*page 212*), or 1 thawed (16-ounce) frozen Sara Lee All-Butter Pound Cake, cut into ¾-inch-thick slices

This dish was created when I competed on Food Network's Chopped: Grill Masters. *When I opened the "mystery basket," the only ingredients I recognized were pound cake and quail eggs. This took me back to Sundays after church in the summer when Mama made pound cake, strawberries, and ice cream. An Oklahoma summer could melt that ice cream quicker than you could eat it, but that's what made it so good. On* Chopped, *I knew I didn't have enough time to make ice cream, but I wanted to re-create that perfect moment when ice cream melts on cake to make a sweet glaze. Mama always taught us to improvise and stick to our roots.*

1. Place the berries in a small bowl and combine with 2 to 4 tablespoons of the sugar. Set aside.

2. In a small bowl, combine the remaining ⅓ cup sugar, the cream, egg, and vanilla. Beat until the batter thickens just slightly.

3. In a 12-inch cast iron skillet, melt 1 tablespoon of the butter over medium heat. Place 4 or 5 pieces of the cake in the skillet and baste the tops with about a tablespoon of the cream batter. Flip and repeat. Continue cooking the cake until lightly toasted, about 2 minutes per side. Be sure to flip and coat the cake 2 to 3 more times, allowing it to soak in more of the batter. Reduce the heat to medium-low if necessary. Cool on a wire rack.

4. Add the remaining 1 tablespoon butter to the skillet and repeat with the remaining cake slices.

TIP: You can also grill the pound cake over low to medium heat, as I did on *Chopped*. You can also use about 4 cups of fresh mixed berries in place of the frozen.

5. Top a slice of the cake with about 2 tablespoons of the berries. Place another slice on top to create a sandwich. Top with a tablespoon of the berries and lightly drizzle with some of the remaining cream batter. Note: You may not end up using all of the cream batter.

LEMON-ALMOND POUND CAKE

Pound cake is always a good dessert, because who doesn't like butter? This pound cake has an almond and citrus blend along with the rich taste of butter. Enjoy it alone or in "Ice Cream" Pound Cake with Mixed Berries on page 210.

PREP TIME: 10 MINUTES

TOTAL TIME: 1 HOUR AND 40 MINUTES

MAKES 8 OR 10 SERVINGS

2 sticks butter, softened

2 cups sugar

5 large eggs

1 tablespoon honey

1 tablespoon lemon juice

1 teaspoon vanilla extract

½ teaspoon almond extract

½ teaspoon salt

¼ teaspoon nutmeg

2 cups all-purpose flour

1. Preheat the oven to 350°F with a rack in the middle. Butter and flour a 9-x-5-x-2-inch loaf pan.

2. In a large bowl, cream the butter and sugar together until light and fluffy. Slowly beat in the eggs, one at a time.

3. Beat in the honey, lemon juice, vanilla and almond extracts, salt, and nutmeg until combined. Slowly beat in the flour until combined.

4. Scrape the batter into the loaf pan.

5. Bake for about 1 hour and 30 minutes, or until a toothpick inserted in the center nearly comes out clean. Because this is a dense, thick cake, feel free to make a judgment call about the baking time, and it will set up slightly as it cools.

6. Let the cake cool before removing from the pan. Serve at room temperature.

TIP: If the top begins to brown too quickly you can cover with a piece of tin foil and continue baking.

CHOCOLATE CHIP– KAHLÚA CAKE

PREP TIME: 5 MINUTES

TOTAL TIME: 1 HOUR

MAKES 1 BUNDT CAKE

(12 TO 16 SERVINGS)

---

1 (15.25-ounce) box chocolate fudge cake mix

2 cups sour cream

¾ cup Kahlúa

¼ cup vegetable oil

2 large eggs

6 ounces semisweet chocolate chips

Powdered sugar for sprinkling

This cake would send Willy Wonka into a chocolate coma. I'm a big fan of boxed cake recipes, because most of the hard work is already done for you. Take a rich fudge cake mix, add in a little Kahlúa, and you've got a decadent dessert to share with family and friends.

1. Preheat the oven to 350°F with a rack in the middle. Butter and flour a Bundt pan.

2. In a large bowl, beat the cake mix, sour cream, Kahlúa, oil, and eggs together. Stir in the chocolate chips.

3. Scrape the batter into the Bundt pan. Bake for 45 to 55 minutes, or until a toothpick inserted comes out clean.

4. Let the cake cool before removing from the pan. Cool, then sift powdered sugar over the top and serve at room temperature.

Cattle, horses, dogs, and children all require patience and love.

JAN'S SPICED WINE CAKE

PREP TIME: 10 MINUTES

TOTAL TIME: 55 MINUTES

MAKES 1 BUNDT CAKE

(12 TO 16 SERVINGS)

1 (15.25-ounce) box yellow cake mix

1 (3.4-ounce) package vanilla pudding mix

3 tablespoons all-purpose flour

¾ cup vegetable oil

¾ cup dry white wine or apple juice

5 large eggs

½ teaspoon cinnamon

Powdered sugar for sprinkling

Basque shepherds migrated from the Pyrenees and settled in Nevada and Idaho. This Basque recipe came to us from our friend Jan from Elko, Nevada. Jan brought the cake over to the house once, and I think it was the only thing I ate that night. Five eggs create a rich, moist cake with a note of spice from cinnamon. It's a go-to when we have to bring a dessert to any function.

1. Preheat the oven to 350°F with a rack in the middle. Butter and flour a Bundt pan.

2. In a large bowl, beat the cake mix, pudding mix, flour, oil, and wine or apple juice together until blended.

3. Slowly beat in the eggs, one at a time. Mix in the cinnamon.

4. Pour the batter into the Bundt pan. Bake for 45 minutes, or until a toothpick inserted comes out clean. Allow the cake to cool completely before running a knife along the edge and turning out onto a towel or plate.

5. Generously sprinkle with powdered sugar and serve at room temperature.

The smoothest road will get you there faster, but a rough road will build character.

HOT CHOCOLATE HORSEY CAKE

PREP TIME: 15 MINUTES
TOTAL TIME: 35 MINUTES
MAKES ONE 9-X-13-INCH CAKE
(12 TO 15 SERVINGS)

2 cups all-purpose flour

2 cups sugar

1 teaspoon baking soda

½ teaspoon salt

¾ cup water

½ stick butter

4 heaping tablespoons
unsweetened cocoa

2 large eggs

⅓ cup sour cream

2 heaping teaspoons prepared
horseradish

1 teaspoon vanilla extract

Frosting (*recipe follows*)

My wife says one of the best cakes she ever had was at an Asian restaurant in Ireland, where a chocolate cake with wasabi was served. Now I don't know who that wasabi feller is, but from what I understand, he's got quite a kick to him. She got to piddlin' around in the kitchen, but instead of using wasabi, she added some horseradish, which gives the same subtle heat that will sneak up on you but isn't overpowering. Try this rich dessert for a different twist on chocolate.

1. Preheat the oven to 350°F. Butter a 9-x-13-inch baking pan.

2. In a large bowl, combine the flour, sugar, baking soda, and salt. Set aside.

3. In a small saucepan, combine the water, butter, and cocoa. Cook over high heat until it comes to a boil, stirring occasionally.

4. Slowly beat the cocoa mixture into the flour mixture just until blended.

5. Beat in the eggs, sour cream, horseradish, and vanilla until well mixed.

6. Scrape the batter into the pan. Bake for 20 minutes, or until a toothpick inserted in the center comes out clean. Let cool to room temperature, spread with the frosting, and serve.

FROSTING

PREP TIME: 5 MINUTES
TOTAL TIME: 5 MINUTES
MAKES ABOUT 1 ¾ CUPS

½ stick butter, softened

⅓ cup unsweetened cocoa

3 tablespoons milk

2 cups powdered sugar

1 teaspoon prepared
horseradish

⅛ teaspoon cayenne pepper
(*optional*)

1 teaspoon vanilla extract

1. In a large bowl, beat together the butter and cocoa with an electric mixer until fluffy.

2. Slowly beat in the milk, sugar, horseradish, cayenne pepper, and vanilla until smooth.

Sometimes it's not about the accommodations but the company we keep.

GOOEY MARSHMALLOW CHOCOLATE CAKE

PREP TIME: 20 MINUTES
TOTAL TIME: I HOUR
MAKES I LAYER CAKE
(12 TO 16 SERVINGS)

2 ½ cups all-purpose flour

2 cups sugar

5 tablespoons unsweetened cocoa

I teaspoon baking powder

¼ teaspoon salt

I cup buttermilk

2 large eggs

I cup vegetable oil

I teaspoon vanilla extract

2 teaspoons baking soda

I cup hot water

I (7-ounce) jar marshmallow cream

I cup shredded coconut (*optional*)

Chocolate Frosting (*recipe follows*)

You better break out a new package of napkins for this sweet, gooey goodness. The chocolate cake came from my Aunt Ola, and it was the first cake I ever made. It can sure stand on its own, but I wanted to dress it up a tad with a hint of coconut and some sweetness from marshmallow cream. This is a good cake to make with the young'uns.

1. Preheat the oven to 350°F with racks in the middle and upper third. Butter and flour two 8- or 9-inch cake pans.

2. In a large bowl, combine the flour, sugar, cocoa, baking powder, and salt. Slowly beat in the buttermilk, eggs, oil, and vanilla until combined.

3. In a small bowl, dissolve the baking soda in the hot water. Beat the mixture into the batter.

4. Divide the batter evenly between the cake pans. Bake for 30 to 40 minutes, until a toothpick inserted in the center comes out clean. Let the cakes cool. Run a knife around the sides and remove from the pans.

5. Microwave the marshmallow cream for 10 to 20 seconds to soften slightly. Spread the cream over the top of one cake. Sprinkle with ½ cup of the coconut, if using.

6. Place the second cake on top of the first. Pour the chocolate frosting in the middle and spread out toward the sides with a table knife.

7. Top with the remaining ½ cup of coconut flakes, if using. The frosting and marshmallow will drip down the sides of the cake for a rich, deliciously gooey dessert.

CHOCOLATE FROSTING

PREP TIME: 10 MINUTES
TOTAL TIME: 10 MINUTES
MAKES ABOUT 1¼ CUPS

¼ cup milk

¼ cup unsweetened cocoa

½ stick butter, softened and cut into pieces

1 teaspoon vanilla extract

2½ cups powdered sugar

1. In a medium saucepan, combine the milk and cocoa.

2. Cook the mixture over medium heat until hot, whisking constantly.

3. Add the butter and continue cooking until it melts, stirring constantly.

4. Remove from the heat and whisk in the vanilla. Whisk in the powdered sugar until smooth. Let cool to warm or room temperature before spreading.

You better break out a new package of napkins for this sweet, gooey goodness.

COWBOY COCONUT CAKE

PREP TIME: 5 MINUTES
TOTAL TIME: 50 MINUTES
MAKES ONE 9-X-13-INCH CAKE
(12 TO 15 SERVINGS)

1 (15.25-ounce) box white cake mix

1 (15-ounce) can cream of coconut such as Coco López

1 (8-ounce) tub Cool Whip Whipped Topping

1 cup shredded coconut

I know coconut doesn't seem cowboy, but let me tell you, when it's 112 degrees outside and I'm cooking for a branding, everyone is thinking tropical, cool, and sweet. Call us dreamers, or maybe this was a mirage, but when I fixed this on a ranch, some of those fellers told me it was like going on a vacation to the beach. I told them our situation did have one thing in common with the beach, and that was when we're getting sand in places we didn't want it! So, folks, put on your swim trunks and enjoy this easy island cake—wherever you are.

1. Preheat the oven to 350°F with a rack in the middle. Butter a 9-x-13-inch baking pan.

2. Prepare and bake the cake according to the directions on the box.

3. Meanwhile, pour the cream of coconut into a small bowl and whisk until smooth.

4. Remove the cake from the oven and poke a generous number of holes throughout the cake using a table knife.

5. Pour the cream of coconut over the warm cake. Let the cake cool.

6. Before serving, take the Cool Whip out of the freezer and let it warm up just slightly so it is easy to spread. Spread it evenly over the cake and sprinkle with the coconut flakes. Serve immediately.

CARAMEL-APPLE CINNAMON CUPS

PREP TIME: 45 MINUTES
**TOTAL TIME: I HOUR AND
5 MINUTES**
MAKES 12 SERVINGS

**Puffed Buttery Crust
(page 234), rolled out to
⅛ inch thick**

Stewed Apples (page 193)

**Caramel Sauce
(recipe follows)**

With a rich, buttery crust and caramel sauce, this is a harvest favorite and a great dessert to whip up on a cool autumn day. And if it were me, I'd add some vanilla ice cream and call it supper too!

1. Preheat the oven to 350°F. Butter a 12-cup muffin pan.

2. Cut the rolled-out dough into twelve 4- to 4½-inch circles. Fit the circles in the muffin pan, pushing up the sides and over the top edges.

3. Fill the cups with the stewed apples, allotting about 1½ to 2 tablespoons per cup. (You may not need all the apples.)

4. Bake for 20 to 25 minutes, or until light brown and crisp.

5. Remove from the oven and let cool slightly before removing from the pan. Drizzle with the caramel sauce and serve warm.

A fire will warm your body, but a good friend will warm your heart.

CARAMEL SAUCE

PREP TIME: 10 MINUTES
TOTAL TIME: 10 MINUTES
MAKES ABOUT ¾ CUP

2 teaspoons cornstarch

¼ cup water

I stick butter

¾ cup heavy cream

¼ cup light brown sugar

I tablespoon sugar

I teaspoon vanilla extract

1. In a small bowl, combine the cornstarch and water. Set aside.

2. Melt the butter over medium-low heat in a small saucepan.

3. In a small bowl, mix together the cream, brown sugar, sugar, and vanilla until smooth. Pour into the melted butter.

4. Bring the mixture to a boil, stirring constantly. Add the cornstarch mixture and continue stirring until thick, about 2 minutes.

Caramel-Apple Cinnamon Cups, page 223

SPICED PUMPKIN ROLL WITH CREAM CHEESE FILLING

---•·•·•---

PREP TIME: 55 MINUTES
**TOTAL TIME: 2 HOURS AND
55 MINUTES**
**MAKES I ROLL (ABOUT
8 SERVINGS)**

---•·•·•---

¾ cup all-purpose flour

I teaspoon baking powder

2 teaspoons cinnamon

I teaspoon ginger

½ teaspoon nutmeg

½ teaspoon salt

3 large eggs

I cup sugar

⅔ cup canned pumpkin
(without pumpkin pie spices)

I teaspoon lemon juice

I cup finely chopped pecans
(*optional*)

I to 2 cups powdered sugar

Cream Cheese Filling
(*recipe follows*)

When I was little and we went over to the neighbor's house for a visit, Mama would take a dessert, and this was usually it. It's colorful and a seasonal favorite. And if Mama didn't bring it, her best friend Wandi would have one already waiting. A spiced cake with the flavor of pumpkin pie rolled around a classic cream cheese frosting, it's a great alternative if you're looking for a change from the same ole pumpkin pie.

1. Preheat the oven to 375°F with a rack in the middle. Butter a 10-x-15-inch baking sheet.

2. In a medium bowl, combine the flour, baking powder, cinnamon, ginger, nutmeg, and salt. Set aside.

3. In a large bowl, beat the eggs together for 3 minutes. Slowly beat in the sugar.

4. Stir in the pumpkin and lemon juice until well mixed. Slowly stir in the flour mixture until combined.

5. Pour the batter onto the baking sheet. Sprinkle over the nuts, if using.

6. Bake for 10 to 15 minutes, or until a toothpick inserted in the center comes out clean.

7. Sprinkle a tea towel with enough powdered sugar to cover it. Run a knife around the sides of the cake to loosen it and turn it out onto the towel. Beginning with the narrow end, roll up the warm cake and towel together. Let cool completely.

8. Unroll the towel and cake. Spread the cream cheese filling evenly over the cake. Without the towel, roll the cake back up, starting from the narrow end. Sprinkle with

CREAM CHEESE FILLING

PREP TIME: 5 MINUTES
TOTAL TIME: 5 MINUTES
MAKES ABOUT 1½ CUPS

---

1 (8-ounce) block cream cheese, softened

1 cup powdered sugar

½ stick butter, melted

½ teaspoon vanilla extract

additional powdered sugar to lightly coat the top. Serve at room temperature or cover and place in the icebox for 2 hours, or until chilled. Cut into about 1½-inch-thick pieces and serve.

FOR THE CREAM CHEESE FILLING

In a medium bowl, beat all the ingredients together until smooth.

HORSESHOES IN HEAVEN

He was covered all in sweat,
As I tied my old horse there in the shade.
He said, "An old horse that will stand more than
   five minutes,
Oh, there ain't never been one made."

He wore an old ragged pair of leggings,
That had been cut off just below the knees.
His old hands were hard and callused,
And his arms were like two limbs of a giant oak
   tree.

He said, "You reckon you could hold this old
   feller?
He seems to have a lot of trouble standing still.
Why you'd think after forty-five years of doing
   this,
I'd had enough and got my fill.

"Trimming and shoeing these old horses,
Is sort of like dealing with life.
If you do it with pride and honesty
You'll get through the times of trouble and strife."

With that shoe in hand and a mouth full of nails,
He went back and resumed his chore.
"Pick it up, Old Feller," he mumbled,
"We just like this one and then one more."

Well, he nailed that shoe on pretty quick,
And never missed his aim.
He said, "Sometimes in life you really have to
   struggle,
If there's going to be any kind of gain.

"Take that old anvil there,
That I use to shape the shoes.
Sometimes in life we've all got to have a little
   adjusting,
To keep us straight, to keep us true.

"It's just like everyday living,
'Cause sometimes you don't get a fair deal.
Some of these horses are pretty good,
And some act awful ill."

Well, I watched him untie this old horse,
His back still slightly bent.
And in my mind I wondered about the many
   hours,
Under an old horse's belly that he had really
   spent.

By now his old shirt was salted down,
And soaked by the summer sun.
And it didn't take him long a-trimming,
And my old horse was done.

I thanked him for his story,
And I paid him for his time.
And as I was riding away I could hear his old
   anvil,
Ringing and making a perfect chime.

Well, there ain't a day that went by,
That I didn't think of him and his advice.
And I'd usually stop by and see him every week,
Sometimes more than twice.

But now the horses,
They ain't lined up no more.
His old anvil just sets there silent,
And his leggings lay empty on the floor.

Yeah, sometimes I go to wondering,
And it makes me feel sort of sad.
But the good Lord needed a farrier,
And He got the best one when he hired my dad.

FIRST-NIGHT TROPICAL PIE

PREP TIME: 10 MINUTES

TOTAL TIME: 3 HOURS AND
10 MINUTES

MAKES ONE 9-INCH PIE

1 (21-ounce) can cherry pie
filling

2 (3.4-ounce) boxes vanilla
pudding mix

2 cups crushed pineapple in
juice (from one 20-ounce can)

1¼ cups sour cream

1 (9-inch) store-bought graham
cracker piecrust

½ cup shredded coconut

TIP: If it's hot enough that
even the cacti are sweating,
stick this pie in the freezer
for a frozen treat.

On most of the ranches I've cooked for, we move into camp on Sunday afternoon, and I prepare the first night's supper meal. Between setting up the wagon and teepee, getting my kitchen in order, and cooking for the cowboys—all in about a four-hour span—the day is a little rushed. I like to spoil a good crew by making dessert noon and night, and the first evening is no different. This dessert is a blend of pie and pudding, with tropical flavors that sure are good after a hot day of chasing cows or building fences—and the boys never guess how quick and easy it is.

1. In a large bowl, combine the cherry pie filling and pudding mix. Stir in the crushed pineapple and juice and the sour cream until completely combined.

2. Spread the mixture evenly in the piecrust. Sprinkle with the coconut.

3. Cover and chill in the icebox for at least 3 hours before serving.

BUTTERMILK PIE

PREP TIME: 10 MINUTES
TOTAL TIME: 1 HOUR
MAKES ONE 9-INCH PIE

3 large eggs, beaten

¼ cup all-purpose flour

2 cups sugar

1 stick butter, melted

1 cup buttermilk

1 teaspoon vanilla extract

1 piecrust, unbaked
(store-bought or Sourdough
Piecrust, *page 235*)

This recipe has been on our table for generations, and my son Jeff could eat the whole thing in one sitting. It's quick and simple with only a few ingredients, none of which require a trip to the store. The pie bakes up similar to a creamy custard with a subtle sweetness.

1. Preheat the oven to 350°F. Butter a 9-inch pie pan.

2. In a large bowl, whisk together the eggs, flour, and sugar until smooth.

3. Whisk in the butter, buttermilk, and vanilla until well mixed.

4. Fit the piecrust into the pan. Pour in the buttermilk mixture.

5. Bake for 40 to 50 minutes, or until a toothpick inserted in the center comes out nearly clean. The crust should be golden brown; you may want to cover the edges with tin foil to prevent it from browning too much. Let cool slightly. Serve warm or chilled.

Getting a job done is like building a fire: First you have to start it.

CHERRY TURNOVERS WITH CHOCOLATE-BOURBON DRIZZLE

PREP TIME: 25 MINUTES (INCLUDES DOUGH)
TOTAL TIME: 50 MINUTES
MAKES ABOUT 8 TURNOVERS

1 (21-ounce) can cherry pie filling

1 (8-ounce) block cream cheese, softened

3 tablespoons sugar

1½ teaspoons almond extract

Puffed Buttery Crust (*page 234*), rolled out ¼ to ⅛ inch thick

Chocolate-Bourbon Drizzle (*recipe follows*)

What's a guy to do when he's on a ranch and the works have gone two days over and groceries are running low? I'm sure not going to sacrifice having dessert just because the pantry is bare. Some fruit pie filling and cream cheese wrapped in a flaky pocket will do the trick! And I'm not one to miss an opportunity to throw a little bourbon into the mix, which goes well with semisweet chocolate. Try this with blueberry filling too.

1. Preheat the oven to 350°F. Butter a baking sheet.

2. In a medium bowl, beat together the pie filling, cream cheese, sugar, and almond extract until combined. Set aside.

3. Cut the rolled-out dough into 5½-inch circles. (I use a small bowl or Crisco lid for the circles.)

4. Spoon the cherry mixture evenly in the middle of each circle. Fold over and crimp the edges together with a fork or your fingers.

5. Place the turnovers on the baking sheet and bake for 20 to 25 minutes, or until golden brown.

6. Top with the Chocolate-Bourbon Drizzle and serve warm or at room temperature.

CHOCOLATE-BOURBON DRIZZLE

PREP TIME: 15 MINUTES
TOTAL TIME: 15 MINUTES
MAKES ABOUT 2 CUPS

1 cup semisweet chocolate chips

2 tablespoons butter

1 cup heavy cream

1 teaspoon vanilla extract

¼ cup bourbon

TIP: For a more mellow bourbon flavor, bring the sauce to a boil for 1 to 2 minutes.

1. In a medium bowl set over a saucepan of simmering water, melt the chocolate.

2. Meanwhile, in a small saucepan, melt the butter over medium heat. Stir in the cream and continue cooking until warm.

3. Pour the chocolate into the cream mixture. Add the vanilla and continue cooking, stirring constantly, until the sauce thickens slightly, about 4 minutes.

4. Remove from the heat and whisk in the bourbon. Serve immediately.

COWBOY FRY BREAD

PREP TIME: 10 MINUTES
TOTAL TIME: 1 HOUR AND
20 MINUTES
MAKES 15 TO 20 DOUGHNUT
HOLES

1 (¼-ounce) package
rapid-rise yeast

¼ cup water

1 cup warm milk

1 large egg, beaten

2 tablespoons sugar

1 teaspoon salt

3 cups all-purpose flour

Vegetable oil for frying

Krispy Kreme doesn't deliver out where we're at, so one of the biggest treats for cowboys is when I make doughnuts. If it's a good crew I sure don't mind spoiling them. The reason I like this fry bread is because it isn't too sweet and won't overpower what you put on it. I like to top them with powdered sugar, honey, and/ or cinnamon, or spread with icing. I will also flatten the dough into small circles and top with fruit pie filling. So get in the kitchen and get creative!

1. In a medium bowl, dissolve the yeast in the warm water.

2. Mix in the milk, egg, sugar, and salt. Stir in the flour.

3. Cover with a tea towel and let rise in a warm place for 1 hour, or until nearly doubled in size.

4. Pour 2 to 3 inches of vegetable oil into a medium saucepan. Warm the oil over medium-high heat until the temperature reaches about 325°F to 340°F.

5. Pinch off about 2-inch balls from the dough. Slightly flatten one piece in your hands and place in the oil. Repeat, frying 4 or 5 pieces at the same time. Fry for 1 to 2 minutes on each side, or until golden brown. Remove from the oil and let cool slightly on a paper towel. Repeat with the remaining dough. Serve warm or at room temperature.

PUFFED BUTTERY CRUST

PREP TIME: 10 MINUTES

TOTAL TIME: 10 MINUTES

MAKES ENOUGH FOR 8
TURNOVERS OR 12 APPLE CUPS

2 ¾ cups all-purpose flour

⅓ cup sugar

5 teaspoons baking powder

2 sticks butter, chilled

1 to 1 ¾ cups water

Sure, store-bought crusts are easy, and I'm not opposed to using them. But if you want a truly homemade taste, this is the best crust to pair with something sweet. My grandmother always used to say, "I'd hate to hide my crust with the filling that was in it." This bakes into a delicate, puffy crust with a generous flavoring of butter, much like shortbread. Use for Cherry Turnovers with Chocolate-Bourbon Drizzle (page 232) and Caramel-Apple Cinnamon Cups (page 223).

1. In a large bowl, combine the flour, sugar, and baking powder. Cut in the butter with a fork or pastry cutter until it becomes crumbly.

2. Slowly stir in the water until it forms a soft dough. Turn the dough out onto a lightly floured surface. Lightly work the dough with the flour to remove any stickiness.

SOURDOUGH PIECRUST

PREP TIME: 15 MINUTES

TOTAL TIME: 25 MINUTES

MAKES TWO 9-INCH CRUSTS

2½ cups all-purpose flour

2½ tablespoons sugar

1 teaspoon baking powder

1 teaspoon cinnamon (*optional*)

1 teaspoon salt

1 cup lard or shortening

¾ to 1 cup Sourdough Starter
(*page 34*)

When Grandma gave me the job of cutting lard into flour with a fork, she would say, "It has to be just right, sort of like cracker crumbs." That's when I learned a valuable lesson: In measuring, start with a little and then add more if you need it. This crust has nice flaky layers. Use with your favorite recipe or Buttermilk Pie (page 231) or Strawberry Balsamic Pie (page 238).

1. Preheat the oven to 400°F. Lightly butter a 9-inch pie pan.

2. In a large bowl, mix together the flour, sugar, baking powder, cinnamon (if using), and salt.

3. Cut the lard into the flour mixture with a fork or pastry cutter until it becomes crumbly, like cracker crumbs.

4. Slowly stir in the starter, ¼ cup at a time, until it forms a soft dough. To ensure a flaky crust, add just enough starter to bring the dough together. On a lightly floured surface, lightly knead any stickiness out of the dough. Divide the dough into 2 pieces.

5. Roll the dough out to a 12-inch round ¼ to ⅛ inch thick. Fit into a 9-inch pie pan.

6. To bake, line the dough with tin foil and fill with dry beans or rice. Bake for 15 to 20 minutes, then carefully remove the foil with the beans or rice and bake for 3 to 5 minutes more or until golden brown and set. Or use with any pie recipe and bake according to the recipe's directions and until the crust is golden brown and set.

CHOCOLATE PECAN PIE

PREP TIME: 10 MINUTES
TOTAL TIME: 1 HOUR
MAKES ONE 9-INCH PIE

1½ cups sugar

3½ tablespoons unsweetened cocoa

1 tablespoon all-purpose flour

1 tablespoon cornmeal

¼ teaspoon salt

3 large eggs

½ cup milk

3 tablespoons butter, melted

1 teaspoon vanilla extract

½ cup chopped pecans

1 unbaked piecrust (store-bought or Sourdough Piecrust, *page 235*), fit into a 9-inch pie pan

We always had two pies on our Thanksgiving table: chocolate and pecan. But due to a busy schedule and a lot of hungry mouths, Mama decided to combine them, so now you can have the best of both worlds in one bite. This twist on a holiday classic has a rich, dark taste and a crisp crust, and you'll save time making it.

1. Preheat the oven to 350°F.

2. In a large bowl, whisk together the sugar, cocoa, flour, cornmeal, and salt. Set aside.

3. In a medium bowl, whisk together the eggs, milk, butter, and vanilla.

4. Slowly pour the egg mixture into the dry mixture and whisk well until combined. Stir in the pecans.

5. Pour the filling into the unbaked piecrust.

6. Bake for 45 to 50 minutes, or until a crust develops on the filling and it feels like a set pudding when touched. Serve warm or at room temperature.

TIP: When the edge of the piecrust begins to brown, cover it with foil to prevent it from burning while the pie continues to bake.

YOU-AIN'T-GOIN'-TO-BELIEVE-THIS STRAWBERRY BALSAMIC PIE

◆ ◆ ◆ ◆

PREP TIME: 40 MINUTES
TOTAL TIME: 2 HOURS AND
40 MINUTES
MAKES ONE 9-INCH PIE

◆ ◆ ◆ ◆

3 large eggs

½ cup heavy cream

I teaspoon vanilla extract

I cup plus I tablespoon sugar

3 tablespoons cornstarch

½ cup light brown sugar

½ stick butter, melted

3 tablespoons balsamic vinegar

I cup water

I cup strawberries, cut into
bite-sized pieces

I 9-inch baked piecrust
(store-bought or Sourdough
Piecrust, *page 235*)

*Every good cowboy story starts with, "You ain't goin'
to believe this. . . ." The story may start out a little odd,
but hold on, because in the end it's going to be epic. It's
a lot like this pie. I'm sure you're thinking, "Strawberries and vinegar? It just ain't going to work!" Well,
sometimes opposites attract and make a happy union.
The tang of balsamic vinegar brings out the sweetness
of strawberries, and they come together like thick pudding. This combination came from the imagination of
my sweet wife. And as folks say in my country—it's
larrupin' (dang good)!*

1. In a small bowl, whisk together the eggs, cream, vanilla,
¼ cup of the sugar, and the cornstarch. Set aside.

2. In a medium saucepan, combine ¾ cup of the sugar,
the brown sugar, butter, vinegar, and water. Cook over
high heat until the mixture comes to a boil, stirring occasionally. Remove from the heat and let sit for 3 minutes.

3. Very slowly whisk the egg mixture into the saucepan.
Return the saucepan to medium-low heat. Continue cooking for about 5 minutes, stirring constantly, until the mixture thickens almost to a pudding. Let the mixture cool to
warm.

4. Meanwhile, mix the strawberries and the remaining
1 tablespoon of sugar in a small bowl.

5. Drain any moisture from the strawberries and stir into
the pie mixture.

6. Scrape the mixture into the baked piecrust. Serve the
pie warm or at room temperature, or chill it for at least
2 hours before serving. My father-in-law prefers the pie
warm, but I like it chilled.

INDEX